Haunting the Knowledge Economy

This highly original book provides an engaging and critical introduction to the knowledge economy. The knowledge economy is a potent force pervading global and national policy circles. Yet few people outside the field of economics understand its central ideas and practices. This book makes these accessible. But it does much more.

Haunting the Knowledge Economy provokes 'conversations' between the knowledge economy and those marginalized economies that haunt it: the risk, gift, libidinal and survival economies. These illuminate the knowledge economy's shortcomings and point to alternative possible systems of exchange and sets of values. This multi-disciplinary study takes the knowledge economy out of the hands of the economists and brings it into creative tension with the ideas of key thinkers from sociology, anthropology, philosophy and ecology.

Illustrating the benefits of conversing with the ghosts of alternative economies, this provocative book will unsettle the way in which the knowledge economy is understood.

Jane Kenway holds a Chair in Global Education Studies in the Education Faculty, Monash University, Australia. Her latest books include her co-authored *Masculinity Beyond the Metropolis* (Palgrave/Macmillan 2006) and *Consuming Children: Entertainment-Advertising-Education* (Open University Press 2002), co-edited *Innovation and Tradition: the Arts, Humanities and the Knowledge Economy* (Peter Lang 2004) and *Globalizing Education: Policies, Pedagogies, and Politics* (Peter Lang 2005).

Elizabeth Bullen is a Lecturer in the School of Communication and Creative Arts, Faculty of Arts, Deakin University, Australia. Her research interests include gender, globalization and consumption practices. She is co-author of *Consuming Children: Entertainment-Advertising-Education* (Open University Press 2002) and co-editor of *Innovation and Tradition: the Arts, Humanities and the Knowledge Economy* (Peter Lang 2004).

Johannah Fahey is a writer and academic. She is a Research Fellow in the Education Faculty, Monash University, Australia. Her research interests include poststructuralism, postcolonialism, globalization and contemporary Australian visual arts. Her latest book is *Before and Now: David Noonan* (Thames and Hudson 2005). Her forthcoming co-authored book with Jane Kenway is *Globalising the Research Imagination* (Routledge).

Simon Robb is Research Fellow at the Hawke Institute, University of South Australia. His research interests include literary theory and social sustainability. He is co-editor of *Innovation and Tradition: the Arts, Humanities and the Knowledge Economy* (Peter Lang 2004) and author of the experimental history *The Hulk* (Post Taste 2003).

International Library of Sociology
Founded by Karl Mannheim
Editor: John Urry
Lancaster University

Recent publications in this series include:

Risk and Technological Culture
Towards a sociology of virulence
Joost Van Loon

Reconnecting Culture, Technology and Nature
Mike Michael

Advertising Myths
The strange half lives of images and commodities
Anne M. Cronin

Adorno on Popular Culture
Robert R. Witkin

Consuming the Caribbean
From Arwaks to Zombies
Mimi Sheller

Crime and Punishment in Contemporary Culture
Claire Valier

Between Sex and Power
Family in the world, 1900–2000
Goran Therborn

States of Knowledge
The co-production of social science and social order
Shelia Jasanoff

After Method
Mess in social science research
John Law

Brands
Logos of the global economy
Celia Lury

The Culture of Exception
Sociology facing the camp
Bulent Diken and Carsten Bagge Lausten

Visual Worlds
John Hall, Blake Stimson and Lisa Tamiris Becker

Time, Innovation and Mobilities
Travel in technological cultures
Peter Frank Peters

Complexity and Social Movements
Multitudes acting at the edge of chaos
Ian Welsh and Graeme Chesters

Qualitative Complexity
Ecology, cognitive processes and the re-emergence of structures in post-humanist social theory
Chris Jenks and John Smith

Theories of the Information Society, 3rd Edition
Frank Webster

Mediating Nature
Nils Lindahl Elliot

Haunting the Knowledge Economy
Jane Kenway, Elizabeth Bullen, Johannah Fahey with Simon Robb

Haunting the Knowledge Economy

Jane Kenway, Elizabeth Bullen, Johannah Fahey with Simon Robb

Routledge
Taylor & Francis Group
LONDON AND NEW YORK

First published 2006
by Routledge
2 Park Square, Milton Park, Abingdon, Oxon OX14 4RN

Simultaneously published in the USA and Canada
by Routledge
270 Madison Ave, New York, NY 10016

Routledge is an imprint of the Taylor & Francis Group, an informa business

Typeset in Sabon by
Book Now Ltd
Printed and bound in Great Britain by
Antony Rowe Ltd, Chippenham, Wiltshire

British Library Cataloguing in Publication Data
A catalogue record for this book is available from the British Library

Library of Congress Cataloging in Publication Data
A catalog record has been requested

ISBN10: 0–415–37067–1 (hbk)
ISBN10: 0–203–03049–4 (ebk)

ISBN13: 978–0–415–37067–7 (hbk)
ISBN13: 978–0–203–03049–3 (ebk)

Contents

Foreword

The notion of the knowledge economy seems safely a matter for economists, something technical and concerned with the changing character of economies in the twenty-first century. Indeed, many economists and economically-oriented policy-makers have presumed this is the case: that the knowledge economy is predetermined within given economies by endogenous processes that generate growth. However, here and there, it is clear that this cannot be the end of the matter.

There must be something about social and political life that affects these apparently economic mechanisms.

But in this eloquent and beautifully written new book the role of the economist is rolled back still further. A complex genealogy is constructed in which almost all components and elements of the so-called knowledge economy are characterized in terms of Derrida's notion of haunting. These various spectres are rather like the spectre of Marx haunting Europe in the twentieth century. The notion of the knowledge economy is refracted through the alternative ghostly economies of risk, gift, libidinal, and survival that are elaborated in depth.

In a way, the four authors construct a distinct social theory for the twenty-first century. This is derived from empirical material, including qualitative interviews, policy documents and case and cameo studies.

Their theory goes beyond simple distinctions of economic and social life and reveals through careful quotation, discursive analysis, and argument some emerging contours of what elsewhere I call an 'economy of signs'.

And in their economy of signs in this book, the economy is shown to be so deeply interwoven with life, culture, and meaning that it is everywhere, and far too important to be left to economists and their embrace of the thrill of the knowledge economy. Twenty-first century social theory will need to deal with Kenway *et al.*'s important dissection of these various economies, of knowledge, risk, gift, libidinal, and survival. Always remembering that these are never just 'economic', and are too significant to be left to the dismal science, indeed they are often matters of life and death.

John Urry, *Lancaster University*
Series Editor, International Library of Sociology

Acknowledgements

We wish to express our gratitude to the Australian Research Council which funded the three-year Discovery-Project *Knowledge, Economy, Society: a sociological study of an education policy discourse in Australia in globalising circumstances*. This book stems from that project. We would also like to thank the University of South Australia, Monash University, and Deakin University for providing the institutional bases within which to write. We are also grateful to all the people who participated in our interviews. We thank David Noonan for his kind permission to reproduce his image on the cover, and for his design suggestions. Joan Fox provided valuable copyediting and we express our sincere appreciation to her. The Andreas Gursky photographs are courtesy of Monika Spruth Galerie, Koln./Bild-Kunst and Matthew Marks Gallery, New York. Licensed by Viscopy, Sydney 2005. Finally, our families have inspired and supported us always and for that we are very thankful.

Note about the cover

The cover features 'owl wallpaper' from the *Waldhaus* series (2002) by Australian artist David Noonan (see Fahey 2004). The owl is a leitmotif in Noonan's work. He is fascinated with this creature as it is heavily invested with a range of different meanings. The owl's association with the supernatural and the gothic relates to our 'haunting' theme, whilst its connection with wisdom and knowledge links to our engagement with particular forms of knowledge in, and excluded by, the knowledge economy.

Abbreviations

ALPSP	Association of Learned and Professional Society Publishers
ARC	Australian Research Council
CBD	Convention of Biological Diversity
COB	Coalition Against Biopiracy
CORDIS	Community Research and Development Information Service
CRC	Cooperative Research Centre
CSIRO	Commonwealth Scientific and Research Organization
DCMS	Department for Culture, Media and Sport
DEST	Department of Education, Science and Training
ETC	Erosion, Technology and Concentration
ETUCE	European Trade Union Committee for Education
GATS	General Agreement of Trade in Services
GDP	Gross Domestic Product
GNP	Gross National Product
ICFTU	International Confederation of Free Trade Unions
ICT	Information and Communication Technology
IP	Intellectual Property
IPR	Intellectual Property Rights
ISR	Department of Industry, Science and Resources
IT	Information Technology
MICA	Ministry of Information, Communications and the Arts
NGO	Non-government Organization
NOIE	National Office of the Information Economy
OA	Open Access
OECD	Organisation for Economic Co-operation and Development
OSI	Open Society Institute
QUT	Queensland University of Technology
R&D	Research and Development
RCUK	Research Councils United Kingdom
SPARC	Scholarly Publishing and Academic Resources Coalition
SPRU	Science Policy Research Unit
TC&A	Tissue Culture and Art Project

TRIPS	Trade-Related Intellectual Property Rights
TUAC	Trade Union Advisory Committee
TWN	Third World Network
UNESCO	United Nations Educational, Scientific and Cultural Organization
WIPO	World Intellectual Property Organization
WTO	World Trade Organization

Foreshadowing

> The air filled with phantoms, wandering hither and thither in restless haste, and moaning as they went. Every one of them wore chains like Marley's Ghost; some few (they might be guilty governments) were linked together; none were free ... The misery with them all was, clearly, that they sought to interfere, for good, in human matters, and had lost the power for ever.
>
> (Dickens, *A Christmas Carol*, [1843] 2003: 52)

Dickens' ghosts

Early in Charles Dickens' *A Christmas Carol* (1843), the ghost of his former business partner, Jacob Marley, appears before Ebenezer Scrooge. The purpose of the spectre's arrival on this bleak Christmas Eve is to herald the coming of three spirits: the Ghost of Christmas Past, the Ghost of Christmas Present, and the Ghost of Christmas Future. The purpose of the Christmas ghosts is to show Scrooge the cost of living a life circumscribed by economic interests. He is the personification of capitalism, measuring the value of his lonely life solely in terms of monetary profits and losses. As such, he is liable to the fate that has befallen Marley. Like the phantoms that fill the air, Marley's ghost is bound in chains, decorated with 'cash-boxes, keys, padlocks, ledgers, deeds, and heavy purses wrought in steel' (Dickens [1843] 2003: 44), these chains signify a bondage to capitalism. The overt purpose of the ghosts in *A Christmas Carol* is to teach Scrooge how to live his life in a more kindly and kindred way.

In the Preface to *A Christmas Carol*, Dickens states that he has 'endeavoured in this Ghostly little book, to raise the Ghost of an Idea'. The ghost that haunts this apparently sentimental Christmas fable has a critical social purpose. The ghosts that haunt Scrooge are also the ghosts that haunt nineteenth-century industrial capitalism, a theme Dickens addresses more directly and fiercely in novels like *Oliver Twist* and *Hard Times*. These economic and social themes continue to have a haunting timbre in the twenty-first century, even though the face of capitalism has altered. Today, mental rather than manual production has become the mainstay of capitalism; the knowledge economy rather than the industrial economy is its cornerstone.

The notion of the knowledge economy made a decisive entry into policy discourses around the globe when the Organisation for Economic Co-operation and Development (OECD) published *The Knowledge-based Economy* (1996). It defines knowledge-based economies as 'economies which are directly based on the production, distribution and use of knowledge and information' (ibid.: 7). The report identifies the indicators of the knowledge-based economy, outlines employment trends, the role of the science system, and the implications for government. In this document, the knowledge-based economy functions as the overarching term that encompasses variant and related notions of the information society, network society, and learning economy. Information and communications technology (ICT) have a pivotal role in all such naming and framing of the global economy.

Since the publication of the OECD report, policy-makers around the world have developed policies that fuse various ideas about the relationship between knowledge, information, learning, the economy, and society (Rooney *et al.* 2003). Such policies identify the rise of knowledge-intensive productivity, the globalization of economic activity, and the networked character of economies and cultures as key features of the global knowledge economy (Castells 1996a; Marginson 2002). The discourse of the knowledge economy and associated discourses have become powerful levers and drivers of policy in such international and supranational bodies as the OECD (2004a) and the European Commission (2003a). They are also used extensively in policy in the USA (2003), UK (2005), Australia (2004), Canada (2002), and Ireland (2005) particularly, and by international organizations assisting developing nations (World Bank 2005). Such policies typically represent knowledge economy initiatives as the way to economic prosperity and scientific and social progress. The knowledge economy is a dominant economic and ideological force in today's world.

Importantly, the term 'economy' cannot be defined simply as a system of exchange. It can also be defined as 'the regulated circulation of values' (Frow 1997: 115). One might well ask, therefore, what values does the knowledge economy circulate and regulate? What are its economic, social, cultural, and ethical values? Which values does it privilege and which does it marginalize? In answering such questions, we, like Dickens, seek to raise 'the Ghost of an idea'. We suggest that the knowledge economy is haunted by the spectres of alternative economies, and that these help to alert one to the knowledge economy's values – its priorities, preferences, limitations, exclusions, contradictions and blind spots.

From Dickens to Derrida

When Dickens wrote *A Christmas Carol* in 1843, the ill effects of industrialization and urbanization were becoming increasingly difficult to ignore. The transition from a stable agricultural and commercial society to a modern industrial society created the factory system of large-scale machine production, a gathering of the labouring population in great urban factory centres, and dramatic changes in the social and economic structure. In the novel, Dickens portrays a haunted atmosphere to create a literary motif that critiques London's socio-economic climate.

Significantly, in the 1840s it is not only the work of Dickens that is troubled by capitalism and haunted by spectres. At this time, both bourgeois reformers and radical politicians were seeking changes in their national governments. In *The Communist Manifesto* (1848), published just prior to the revolutions in Europe, Marx and Engels announce: 'There is a spectre haunting Europe; the spectre of Communism. All the powers of old Europe have entered into a holy alliance to exorcise this spectre' (2002: 1).

In this seminal work, they outline their theory of history and, to put it simply, prophesy an end to the exploitation of the working class (the proletariat) by the ruling capitalists (the bourgeoisie), who are driven by the logic of capitalism to seek ever-greater profits. They believe capitalism contains the seeds of its own destruction, and maintain that communism will evolve (from feudalism to capitalism to socialism) through class struggles between workers and owners of capital. In their opinion, as wealth becomes more concentrated in the hands of fewer capitalists, the ranks of dissatisfied workers will swell, leading to revolution and a classless society. Whilst the capitalist 'alliance' attempts to chase away or banish the ghost of communism, it does not succeed in killing it entirely, and this opens the way for a future communism or a communism that is yet to come. For Marx and Engels, capitalism in the nineteenth century is haunted by the spectre of communism. For Jacques Derrida, capitalism in the late twentieth century is haunted by the spectre of Marx.

Derrida's ghosts

Derrida's title, *Specters of Marx* (1994), deliberately evokes the opening line of *The Communist Manifesto*. In the book, he describes contemporary anti-Marxist attitudes and problematizes the 'new world order' of capitalism. In the Introduction to *Specters of Marx*, Magnus and Cullenberg suggest the central question Derrida seeks to answer is: 'Has the collapse of communism [of which the fall of the Berlin Wall is emblematic] also spelled the death of Marxism?' (1994: viii). Although influential neo-liberals, in particular Francis Fukuyama who wrote *The End of History and the Last Man* (1992), maintain Marxism is dead and hail the triumphs of capitalism, Derrida believes that, despite such assertions and attempts to exorcize the spirit of Marxism, Marxism continues to have a haunting influence. Indeed, *Specters of Marx* is Derrida's 'Marxist' analysis and critique of capitalism, where he invents the term 'hauntology' to refer to the logic of the ghost. In Callari's opinion, 'Derrida has summoned the figure of the ghost to evoke an image of epistemological tremor – the tremor-inducing effect of Marx on European capitalism being the most notable instance' (2002: 248). It is not our intention to give an exhaustive account of the numerous concepts or strands of argument Derrida articulates in *Specters of Marx* (see Laclau 1995; Sprinker 1999). Rather we will focus on his notion of 'hauntology' to provide the theoretical basis for the practice of haunting, illustrated by the ghosts in Dickens' *A Christmas Carol*, and applied to the spectral economies that, we argue, haunt the knowledge economy.

Derrida develops his understanding of ghosts (spectrality) and his theory of haunting (hauntology) by asking: 'what is the *being-there* of a specter? What is the mode of presence of a specter?' (1994: 38, original emphasis). For Derrida, the ghost rattles the very foundations of existence and problematizes an ontology based on presence and informed by Heideggerian philosophy. Ontology establishes existence, or a theory of being, in terms of 'tangible certainty and solidity' (Jameson 1995: 75). Alternatively, Derrida's hauntology – a neologism that deliberately sounds like 'ontology' when pronounced in French – serves to 'underscore the very uncertainties of the spectral itself, which promises nothing tangible in return' (ibid.).

Derrida's notion of hauntology is built on a presence/present double gesture. The ghost confuses our understanding of existence as presence. The ghost *is* but it does not exist. As it is neither present nor absent, it places 'being as presence' in doubt. The ghost also confuses our understanding of time. The ghost leaves traces of the past and the future by conjuring those who are already dead and making prophesies about those who are not yet born. The Ghosts of Christmas Past, Present and Future in Dickens' *A Christmas Carol* are an example. Thus, time is no longer ordered according to a linear progression from the distant past, to the present moment, and into the unforeseen future. The ghost's state of being desynchronizes time. In *A Derrida Dictionary* (2004: 112), Lucy states that when confronted with the spectre, 'all that metaphysics allows or constrains us to regard as certain (concerning time, identity, presence, and so forth) is opened to the risk of becoming uncertain, of coming undone or being disjointed'.

The knowledge economy's ghosts

The knowledge economy is a contemporary and dominant manifestation of capitalism. It is driven by the production, distribution, and consumption of knowledge. Knowledge economy policy discourse, with its interlaced ideas about knowledge, information, learning, economy, and society, has become so influential it has assumed the status of truth, dominating the policy lexicon and excluding alternative economies – even denying that they exist. The existence of the knowledge economy, it seems, is self-evident; its future without doubt. Apparently, we are all moving inexorably towards an economy, and indeed society, determined and dominated by the following principles: techno-science, techno-scientific innovation, the codification of knowledge through ICTs, the commodification of knowledge through intellectual property regimes, and the production and circulation of knowledge by and through instrumental and entrepreneurial knowledge workers and networks. These are the knowledge economy's self-confident but primarily self-referential essences. There is, in knowledge economy discourse, an un-reflexive celebration of the triumphs of contemporary capitalism and a conjuring against the spectres of alternative economies.

According to Derrida, 'ghosts haunt places [discourses, ideologies, etc.] that exist without them; they return to where they have been excluded from' (2000: 152). The ghosts of other, non-market economies haunt the knowledge economy because they undermine its presence and it, in turn, either divests them of meaning or is reluctant to recognize them – indeed, may refuse to do so. Were it to recognize alternative economies, it would be exposed to its own weak spots and blind spots, its own contradictions, its ultimate frailty and moral futility. Yet, denial is precisely the reason for the return of the revenant.

Derrida's logic of hauntology suggests 'the irreducibility of the political understood as that moment where the sedimented meanings of the socio-economic are contested' (Critchley 1995: 7). In other words, the seemingly rock-hard base upon which knowledge economy discourse is built is challenged by the logic of hauntology, and as a result its 'sedimented meanings' start to crumble and collapse. In *Specters of Marx*, Derrida responds to 'the fact that a dogmatics [of capitalism] is attempting to install its worldwide hegemony in paradoxical and suspect conditions' (1994: 51). He maintains that we live in:

> a time when some have the audacity to neo-evangelize in the name of the ideal of a liberal democracy ... [despite the fact that] never have violence, inequality, exclusion, famine, and thus economic oppression affected as many human beings in the history of the earth and humanity.
>
> (Ibid.: 85)

What Derrida is suggesting is that the reality of late-twentieth-century capitalism contradicts its self-justifying, self-protecting, and self-indulgent ideals. One way to draw attention to the contradictions between the dire reality that Derrida describes, and the knowledge economy's version of an ideal world, is to use ghosts to create doubt where there is certainty. Joseph maintains that 'Derrida teaches us that spectres can work for us all and that we can invoke them in order to question any discourse' (2001: 96). In terms of contemporary capitalism, and knowledge economy discourse more specifically, the ghosts of alternative economies arise to draw attention to its inherent instability, to challenge the certainty of its economic dogma by offering alternative perspectives.

As Derrida states: 'haunting belongs to the structure of every hegemony' (1994: 34). Hauntology arrives at that moment when hegemony is 'dark, threatened and threatening' (ibid.: 52). The haunting of the knowledge economy begins as it ascends to the hegemonic zone. Its hegemony involves the fevered celebration of the current order, the disavowal of the before, the after and the minoritarian. But, also, hegemony is a haunted space of counter-hegemonic forces. Where we find the ghosts of the knowledge economy, then, is not only in a critique of the coherency of its discourse, not only in the inconsistencies of its universalities, but also when we begin to re-order that discourse along lines that admit to ambiguity.

Drawing on Derrida, Jameson maintains the ghost makes the solid foundations of the present begin to 'waver'. Its haunting presence draws attention to the fact that the present is not 'as self-sufficient as it claims to be; that we would do well not to count on its density and solidity, which might under exceptional circumstances betray us' (Jameson 1995: 76). The spectres of alternative economies destabilize the seemingly solid foundations of the knowledge economy. These ghosts call the present existence of the knowledge economy into question.

This book is not preoccupied with the ghosts that haunt capitalism *per se*, or indeed those that haunt Dickens, Marx or Derrida, but rather, and more specifically, those spectral economies that haunt the knowledge economy. By acknowledging things that are neither fully present nor fully absent, things that occupy the threshold between the perceptible and the imperceptible, we are able to identify the ghostly economies haunting the knowledge economy. We identify these as the risk, gift, libidinal, and survival economies and discuss them in Chapters 2 to 5.

In explaining such alternative economies' systems of exchange, in elaborating on the values that they regulate and circulate, and in illuminating their haunting practices, we draw on the ideas of some foundational thinkers in the fields of sociology, anthropology, philosophy, and ecology. These are respectively Ulrich Beck, Marcel Mauss, Jean-François Lyotard, and Vandana Shiva. And we juxtapose their work against some of the relevant key concepts in the knowledge economy discourse. Some of the foundational thinkers of the knowledge economy are introduced in Chapter 1. There, we also offer a genealogy of the knowledge economy discourse tracing its convoluted conceptual tributaries and showing how its very own ghosts illuminate its imprecision and partiality – particularly its ideological slippage between economy and society.

Our particular application of Derrida's theory of haunting (hauntology) to the knowledge economy, our conjuring of alternative forms of economy, seeks to take 'the economy' and 'knowledge' out of the hands of the economists. This is largely a conceptual book that connects ideas from across the disciplines and draws from the creative tensions that this evokes. It also weaves through each chapter illustrative examples of its more abstract points. These examples and the broader analysis that informs our discussion of them arise from three main sources. The first source includes policy documents and policy analysis published by various international and supranational governmental organizations and national governments. These allow us to suggest some ways that the knowledge economy discourse is manifest in different policy settings. The second source is interviews (anonymized here) conducted in 2003 with senior staff at the OECD, UNESCO, the European Commission, various international labour organizations (International Confederation of Free Trade Unions, European Trade Union Committee for Education, Trade Union Advisory Committee), and senior policy personnel from various departments in the Australian Commonwealth government (see Appendix 1). In the book as a whole, we introduce each section of each chapter with a direct quotation from these interviews. Our purpose in using these quotations in this manner is not to suggest that these are necessarily the views of the organizations for which these people work. Rather, it is to demonstrate a multiplicity of perspectives amongst specialist policy-makers with regard to the key themes of each chapter. Our use of the quotations is gestural rather than systematic. The third source is cameo studies (small, highly-focused case studies and analyses) of different manifestations of knowledge economy policy and of different genres of commentary on it (see Appendix 2). The illustrative cameo studies offer on-the-ground views of the knowledge economy from the standpoints of those outside its instigating field – from those individuals, groups or institutions who either must, or feel compelled to, respond to its field of force and possible consequences.

Derrida's notion that we must learn to live with ghosts, and be willing to converse with them, leads us to ask the methodological question, what issues might arise if we provoke 'conversations' between the knowledge economy and its other spectral economies? Throughout this book we metaphorically answer this question. We elaborate on what each economy has to say about itself to itself, and about itself to the knowledge economy in the haunting exchange. And we also ask what speaking positions these economies adopt, and what power relationships structure the conversations' questions and responses, noise and silences?

Overall, our central argument is that the unequal but nonetheless salient encounter between the knowledge economy and its ghosts raises critical questions for the knowledge economy and its associated discourses. In Chapter 2 on the risk economy, we ask, in the interests of techno-scientific innovation, what risks does the knowledge economy produce? If the 'ideal' knowledge worker of the knowledge economy is the techno-scientist and the entrepreneur, is their risk persona also ideal or might it be hazardous? Our central questions in Chapter 3 on the gift economy are, is knowledge best thought of in commercial terms or are there benefits to giving it away? What different relationships and responsibilities do commodified and non-commodified knowledges involve and invoke? Chapter 4 on the libidinal economy poses the question, what is the relationship between the knowledge economy and those knowledges it marginalizes? It asks: can the arts' critical libidinal intensities be contained by commerce? Chapter 5 is on the survival economy and the central question here is: what is the relationship between economy, ecology, intellectual property and the survival of the planet's diversity?

Hauntology as a method of inquiry allows us, throughout the book, to identify the knowledge that the knowledge economy privileges, the human subjects it seeks to produce, and the global politics it favours. Hauntology also allows us to ask questions about how the knowledge economy attends to the responsibilities that it has to the past and the future in the present moment. How does it, might it, take responsibility for past and present injustices? How will it affect future knowledge formations, future generations and the future of the planet? What effects will linger beyond the knowledge economy's current incarnation?

1 The knowledge economy

> "You don't believe in me," observed the Ghost.
> "I don't know," said Scrooge.
> "What evidence would you have of my reality, beyond that of your senses?"
> "I don't know," said Scrooge.
> "Why do you doubt your senses?"
> "Because," said Scrooge, "a little thing affects them. A slight disorder of the stomach makes them cheats. You may be an undigested bit of beef, a blob of mustard, a crumb of cheese, a fragment of an underdone potato. There's more of gravy than of grave about you, whatever you are."
>
> (Dickens, *A Christmas Carol*, [1843] 2003: 45)

Scrooge is inclined to dismiss Marley's apparition as a bout of indigestion. When he hears the sound of rattling chains he is startled but initially sceptical: 'It's humbug!' said Scrooge. 'I won't believe it' (Dickens [1843] 2003: 44). When Marley's ghost finally appears before him he still cannot quite believe his eyes. He sees him but remains incredulous, unconvinced that he is really 'there'. His doubt about the ghost's reality points to one significance of hauntology: the spectre is ambiguous; it casts into doubt what we think we know. Derrida (1994: 39) asks, 'What is the time and what is the history of the specter? Is there a present of the specter? Are its comings and goings ordered according to the linear succession of a before and an after … ?' His answer is:

> If there is something like spectrality, there are reasons to doubt [the] reassuring order of presents and, especially, the border between the present, the actual or present reality of the present, and everything opposed to it: absence, non-presence, non-effectivity, inactuality, virtuality, or even the simulacrum in general and so forth. There is first of all the doubtful contemporaneity of the present to itself.
>
> (Ibid.)

In haunting, the ghost disrupts the self-identity of the present – before and after and, therefore, as suggested in Scrooge's speculation about what the ghost is, cause and effect.

The knowledge economy is also an ambiguous and contentious presence in both historical and conceptual terms. Its actual existence, its causes, effects and its relationship to the present are just as difficult to pin down. The knowledge economy, the knowledge-based or -driven economy, knowledge society, information society, and information economy are just a few of a plethora of names used to describe the nature of contemporary economic and associated social change.

Knowledge, information, society, and economy have together become a familiar ensemble of terms that are frequently combined and recombined in various configurations. They are often used interchangeably and uncritically, and are frequently under-defined (Peters 2001) and insufficiently theorized. Whatever the configuration mobilized, they usually have different and illusive meanings over time and in different circles – be they academic, governmental, or international labour organizations. Consider some quick examples from international labour organizations.

Based on his experience at international forums where the information society discourse circulates, a senior staff member in an international trade union organization concluded that, 'Some people tend to be excited by what it [the information society] might be without really having thought it through. So to a lot of people it's a mysterious sort of cloudy concept, which they hope, upon exploring it more deeply, will have more to it than what they currently know.' He goes on to add that 'When people don't have a very realistic idea of what it is, they tend to hype it into something much more than it actually is' (Senior staff member, International Confederation of Free Trade Unions).

At another international labour organization based in Brussels, the term information society is used alongside the terms knowledge economy and learning economy/society.

> We don't have any clear definition or any clear understanding of the meaning of the words. Sometimes we respond to text from the World Bank, from the OECD, from other international organizations and of course we use, on many occasions, the terminology they use and respond to that word. Also on occasions [when] we write our own things, we need to have the words that we know members of the organization understand.
>
> (Senior staff member, Education International)

There is also an understandable resistance to the claims often made about the historical specificity that this set of concepts refers to. As an interviewee from an international labour organization with its headquarters in Paris puts it, 'Looking back in history, my guess is that knowledge at any time was important. Even in the Stone Age period a certain kind of knowledge was required' (Senior staff member, Trade Union Advisory Committee). This small selection of quotations illustrates some of the diverse ways in which our interviewees approach the knowledge economy discourse. Collectively these point to the illusiveness and imprecision of the concepts under scrutiny here.

Such illusiveness and imprecision has led some scholars to dismiss the various combinations of terms associated with knowledge, information, economy, and society as groundless or too vague, global and monolithic, or even as ideological hyperbole (Winston 1998; Webster 1995; May 2002).

Metaphorically, we might say, they regard such concepts, as Scrooge might, as a fragment of potato or an undigested bit of beef – as 'humbug'. However, to debate the existence of the knowledge economy or information society is in some senses beside the point. The fact that these concepts, ill-defined or not, have been taken up in policy means that they are already determinants of social and economic change (Bimber 1995). Or, to put it another way, the knowledge/information economy/society policy discourse is of consequence despite its ambiguity. For this reason, understanding the policy drivers of socio-economic change is critical.

This chapter seeks to provide a resource for such understanding by raising some of the ghosts of this discourse. Our focus is particularly on the ghosts of the knowledge economy policy discourse and we chronicle its evolution and key conceptual tributaries back to the 1960s.

The genealogies of knowledge and information societies/economies are intertwined and tracing their evolution is not easy. The task this chapter undertakes presents a range of methodological difficulties which we will briefly outline. Not least of these is the slippage between concepts and the emergence and disappearance of competing terms and buzzwords. Beniger (1986: 4–5) lists some 75 terms for modern social transformation coined between 1950–84 alone and he himself coins the term 'the control revolution'. He also attributes the coinage of the term information society to Martin and Butler (1981). We will identify an earlier coinage, but hesitate to claim it as the definitive source because, ironically, authoritative information in the information age can be surprisingly difficult to locate and verify.

This is in part due to the fact that the significance of coinage only becomes apparent in retrospect, and in part due to the fact that much of the early literature where these terms appear does not observe academic referencing conventions. Drucker (1969) for instance, in his influential work, does not include a reference list. Contemporary policy documents do not consistently or reliably acknowledge the conceptual origins of the terminology they use, although background papers may provide some of this information. Even scholarly literature is frequently fraught with gaps, absences, and contradictions. While it is commonplace to locate the origin of the knowledge/information economy/society in the work of several key thinkers in the 1960s and to use this as a context for discussion of current usage, it is less common for scholars to track the intervening development of the concepts. Academic discourses are often de-historicized and the coinage of terms or key influences not contextualized in regard to global and local trends or counter-discourses. How and why particular conceptualizations are abandoned or carried forward are frequently ignored. Likewise, while slippage between terms is often acknowledged, the implications are ignored. Is it all merely a matter of semantics or something more?

Scholars have tended to use a range of analytical classifications including disciplinary and theoretical tributaries. Webster (1995: 6), for instance, identifies five analytical definitions of the information society: technological; economic; occupational; spatial; and cultural. He concedes that these criteria are not mutually exclusive, arguing that particular theorists will privilege a particular criterion. We agree. However, this typological approach becomes somewhat strained and artificial when theories are located and analysed accordingly. Such an approach ignores how these different discourses interact and what we might learn from their synergies.

Disciplinary and discursive categories are likewise problematic. There is a tendency to privilege certain discourses over others, for instance economics over futurology or management theory over sociology. The work of futurist and populist writers (Toffler 1980; Naisbitt 1984) tends to be dismissed as 'gee-whiz', 'naïve', 'shallow', and just not 'serious' (Webster 1995). The tendency is to privilege empirical or theory-based sources over more speculative works with a consequent underestimation of the latter's contribution to the durability and popularization of knowledge economy discourses.

In this chapter, we take a chronological approach which, we are aware, imposes a sequence which is necessarily rather more orderly than the reality. Of course, we are conscious that chronology contrasts markedly with hauntology and we will return to this matter at the end of this chapter. However, one of the most intriguing aspects of a chronological approach is that it shows when, under what circumstances, and in what new conceptual robes the revenant returns. Indeed, even though our interviews were conducted in 2003, many of our interviewees have understandings of the knowledge economy discourse that resonate with different historical manifestations of it. They are haunted by a conceptual history that many seem unaware of.

Clearly, we cannot cover the vast literature which has emerged on the subject over the last 50-odd years or, indeed, its multiple conceptual trajectories and manifestations. Some narrowing of focus is always required in overview commentaries such as ours in this chapter. Peters (2003a, 2003b), for instance, focuses on the economics of knowledge, in particular the influence of Hayek (1937, 1945) on the development of neo-liberalism, and on the work of the various Chicago schools of economics. With regard to the economics of knowledge, we, on the other hand, outline the approach of the neo-Schumpeterian school of economics. With a different focus on knowledge itself, David and Foray (2003) draw on the literature relating to the codification of tacit knowledge and the role of ICTs as 'instruments of knowledge' in their treatment of knowledge production. We elaborate on this below, but focus more on the influence of theories of 'Mode 1' and

'Mode 2' knowledge production (Gibbons 1998; Gibbons *et al.* 1994; Nowotny *et al.* 2003). The themes of this chapter have been identified on the basis of what we judge to be the influence, explicit and implicit, of key texts, authors, theories, and concepts on key national and supranational policy documents. We suggest these are critical to defining the knowledge economy and understanding its main drivers and implications.

The origins of the knowledge economy in the 1960s

> While I would not have a specific definition of the drivers of the knowledge-based society, clearly ... knowledge is the raw material for those [countries] with knowledge growth. ... Instead of traditional materials, this is the main ingredient for growth and for social cohesion and this [definition] would probably be shared by most of my colleagues.
>
> (Senior staff member, Policy Development Unit, European Commission: Directorate General for Education and Culture)

In 1956, white-collar workers outnumbered blue-collar workers for the first time in US history. With the benefit of hindsight, futurist John Naisbitt (1984) describes this as one of two milestones that mark the beginning of a globalized 'information society'. His choice of term to describe this nascent 'society' marks his *own* historical location – the term 'information society' did not emerge until later in the 1960s. In fact, the contemporary significance of the change in the constitution of the US labour force was understood in relation to knowledge rather than information. The seeds of the idea of a knowledge society/economy were sown by Professor of Management Peter Drucker (1959), Graduate Business School of New York University, who coined the notions of the 'knowledge worker', 'knowledge work', and 'knowledge industries'. Around the same time, Princeton economist Fritz Machlup undertook a statistical analysis of the production and distribution of knowledge in the US economy, publishing his results in 1962. Machlup calculated that 29 per cent of the gross national product (GNP) derived from knowledge industries, which he broke into five categories: education; research and development (R&D); communications media; information machines (computers); and information services including finance, insurance, and real estate (Beniger 1986: 21–2).

According to Brint (2001: 101–2), Machlup's ideas were popularized by Clark Kerr in his 1963 Godkin Lectures at Harvard, later published as *The Uses of the University* (1963). Here Kerr describes the transformation which universities were undergoing at the time – changes we continue to see today and attribute to knowledge economy policies. These changes include: the education of unprecedented numbers of students; collaboration between industry and education; the adaptation of new intellectual currents; and entrepreneurialism. Kerr (1963: 87–8) argues that the 'growth of the "knowledge industry", which is coming to permeate government and business and to draw into it more and more people raised to higher and higher levels of skill', is basic to this transformation. He claims that 'knowledge' has 'never been so central to the conduct of an entire society' (ibid.: 88), but stops short of describing it as a 'knowledge society'.

Stehr (2001) traces the concept of the knowledge society to Robert E. Lane's (1966) article, 'The decline of politics and ideology in a knowledgeable society', as does Bell (1973). However, according to Jones (1995), it was Drucker's subsequent adoption of Machlup's analysis and the notion of 'knowledge industries' (1969: 263) that led him to coin the phrase 'knowledge economy' in *The Age of Discontinuity* (1969). Drucker also uses the term knowledge society in this book; indeed, he uses it as an overarching concept which encompasses the topics of the knowledge economy, knowledge work and the knowledge worker in the knowledge society. It is notable that he, too, anticipates many of the themes which continue to preoccupy contemporary scholars, educators and policy-makers concerned with the knowledge economy/society. These themes include: the distinction between services and knowledge work; the technological gap (currently referred to as the digital divide); 'brain drain'; the link between education and economic growth; the importance of organizational restructuring; the quantification of knowledge work; the difference between information and knowledge, and, indeed, the question of what knowledge matters in a society in which knowledge is 'the foundation of economy and social action' (ibid.: 350).

The idea of the information society also emerged in the 1960s. May (2000) says it was Fritz Machlup who first coined the term 'information society' in the early 1960s, although he does not reference this claim. Others argue that the term originated in Japan. Castells (1996b: 22) says that 'all terminologies [relating to information] originated in Japan in the mid-60s ... and were transmitted to the West in 1978 by Simon Nora and Alain Minc' – although this latter assertion is contradicted by Bell's (1973) prior usage. Malaguerra *et al.* (2001) suggest that 'information society' was coined as a result of a mistranslation into Japanese of Machlup's *The Production and Distribution of Knowledge in the United States* (1962), but Takagi (1997) claims that Japanese scholar Umesao Tadao used the term in 1960. Morris-Suzuki (1988) offers a less speculative account, pointing to the appearance of the concepts of *jōhōka shakai* or *jōhō shakai* (informational society or information society) in a range of Japanese government and academic papers from 1969 onwards (see, for instance, Yūjirō 1969). Morris-Suzuki links the appearance of the terms with the literature on post-industrial society.

The post-industrial or information society in the 1970s

> When we started out ... we used the term information economy. But that was kind of a reaction to the American term of information superhighway ... And of course in Europe we are more socially conscious.

> Then we used the expression information society, but in reality it's rather the same. ... But maybe we do have a more society application oriented attitude than ... others.
>
> (Senior staff member, European Commission: Directorate General for Information Society)

It is commonplace (Dyer-Witheford 1999; Lyon 1991; Webster 1995) to argue that the concept of the knowledge society and, indeed, the information society, has its roots elsewhere in the literature on post-industrialism of the 1960s and 1970s (Bell 1976; Masuda 1972, 1976, 1980; Touraine 1974) and that it is coterminous with it (Martin 1988). The version theorized by Daniel Bell (first published 1973) is most often referred to, at least by Anglophone commentators.

In sum, Bell claimed information rather than energy is the transforming resource; intellectual capital rather than financial capital is the strategic resource; intelligent technologies and ICTs supersede machine technologies; and a scientific, technical, and professional skill base displaces the semi-skilled worker. When, in *The Coming of Post-industrial Society*, Bell theorized 'post-industrial society', he did so with regard to the emergent and transitional changes of the times and with a focus on technological change (1976: x). He counter-poses post-industrial society and pre-industrial society. In the latter, production is agrarian and centres on the '*extraction*' of natural resources. In industrial society, machine technology and manufacturing is the predominant form of production. According to Bell, post-industrial society 'is one of *processing* in which telecommunications and computers are strategic for the exchange of information and knowledge' (ibid.: xii). In other words, an axial principle is 'intellectual technology' (ibid.: ix–x). Although it does not displace industrial society, gross domestic product (GDP) and employment are increasingly concentrated in the knowledge sectors.

Whereas 'capital and labor are the major structural features of an industrial society, information and knowledge are those of post-industrial society', and this creates vastly different forms of social organization. However, Bell (ibid.: xiii) argues that post-industrialism is not post-capitalism. Post-industrialism is a conceptual schema for socio-technological change – and not socio-economic change. Post-industrial society, Bell (1973: 212) claims, is a 'knowledge society' precisely because 'knowledge and technology are embodied in social institutions and represented by persons'. Ultimately, however, he rejects the notions of a knowledge society and, indeed, information society, which he describes as 'modish' and a 'fashionable wind' (1976: ix).

Bell's contribution to Dertouzos and Moses' edited collection (1979) which he entitled 'The social framework of the Information Society', appears to indicate a change of heart. The turnaround may have something to do with the fact that the collection in which it appears, *The Computer Age*, had its genesis in the 1974 International Federation of Information Processing

Societies Conference. However, we might speculate that Bell's focus on information and telecommunications technology in post-industrial society is more than a matter of editorial constraints. Drawing on economic historian Innis (1951), Bell suggests that new modes of communication mark the transition from one stage of society to the next. He includes television and computer and the variant modes arising from the convergence of information and communications technologies. This leads him to argue that 'the core of the present communications revolution is not a specific technology but the set of concepts represented by the term information theory' (Bell 1979: 169). We also suggest that information theory played a critical role in the ascendancy of notions of the information society, information economy (Porat 1977) and information revolution (Lamberton 1974) in the 1970s and of the information age (Dizard 1982) in the 1980s. Such theory also helped to produce a tendency to conflate knowledge and information.

In information theory (Shannon and Weaver 1964), information is a quantitative measure of communication exchanges, a sort of 'calculus of communications traffic'. As such, 'information has come to denote whatever can be coded for transmission through a channel that connects a source with a receiver, regardless of semantic content' (Roszak 1986: 12). Simply put, information has nothing to do with meaning. Roszak (1986) argues that 'the cult of information' acts to obscure the qualitative differences between data, knowledge and information. He explains that one of the reasons for this conflation lies in the differences between commonsense understandings of information and its restricted meaning in the discipline of information theory. It is likely that commonsense understandings of information have come to be partially informed by this technical meaning as a consequence of the hype surrounding the proliferation and diffusion of ICTs in the 1970s. Although the Internet – as the 'information superhighway' – was not widely available until the early 1990s, VCRs and microprocessors, the Ethernet, pocket calculators, word processors, video games, and the Walkman and cellular phones all became publicly available in the 1970s, at least in the First World. All involve storage, retrieval, and transmission of information.

In many pertinent scholarly discussions in the 1970s, information technologies were privileged over other forms of technology as a factor of economic growth and the terms information society and information economy displaced knowledge-oriented terminology at this time. This may partly be explained by the fact that knowledge was, and remains, notoriously difficult to measure, but information theory insists that 'information is a purely quantitative thing' and thus can be statistically measured (Webster 1995: 25). In 1977, Marc Porat published *The Information Economy*, regarded as a key text in the emergence of both the knowledge and information economy. Although Brint (2001: 105) argues that Porat's conception of the information and knowledge sectors is essentially the same as Machlup's (discussed above), there is a significant difference in the way in which they conceptualize information and knowledge respectively. Machlup (1962: 30) defines knowledge as 'any human (or human-induced) activity effectively designed to create, alter, or confirm in a human mind – one's own or anyone else's – a meaningful appreciation, awareness, cognizance, or consciousness'. Porat (1977: 47), on the other hand, defines information as 'data that have been organized and communicated. The information activity includes all the resources consumed in producing, processing and distributing information goods and services'. At the heart of Porat's definition is the notion of information handling, the manipulation of symbols or symbolic objects which involves the creation of new knowledge at one extreme and routine data processing or codification at the other: the work of ICTs.

Economic crisis and post-Fordist schools of thought in the 1980s

> There is a speedier process of decision-making as well as increased speed regulating the production of goods as well as services and that's where ICT has certainly changed or contributed to changes compared to procedures, production forms [and] methods of the past and of course we see changes affecting skill requirements, employment, employment conditions and working conditions. But I wouldn't say that they are the society completed.
>
> (Senior staff member, Trade Union Advisory Committee)

By the end of the 1970s, a number of national governments had taken steps towards the formation of information society policies, including Japan (Sangyo Kozo Shingikai Joho Sangyo Bukai 1969), France (Nora and Minc 1978) and Canada (Valaskakis 1979). According to Dyer-Witheford (1999: 35), a key impetus for this was the recession of the mid-1970s, although Morris-Suzuki (1988) says that in the Japanese case, the economy had come under strain by the late 1960s. Stagnation in the growth of the developing global economy was attributed to the decline in productivity due to the saturation of mass markets, rising environmental and safety costs, and increased competition in the international marketplace (Watkins 1994). Jones (1995: 34) argues that the resulting high inflation, high unemployment, and slow economic growth were partly compounded by the world oil crisis and 'partly side-effects of the transition to post-industrialism'. This period also marks the so-called 'end' of organized capitalism and Fordist production – an industrial economy typified by mass production and mass marketing (Watkins 1994). Paradoxically, these factors accelerated the transition towards the information society, in which technology promised a solution to the crises of industrialism, and in which 'the idea of an information revolution ... became a crucial intellectual and rhetorical component in a project of high-technology restructuring pursued collaboratively by state and corporate sectors throughout the advanced capitalist world' (Dyer-Witheford 1999: 36).

The information revolution of the 1980s, however, did not necessarily resolve the social and economic problems that had accompanied the 1970s world recession, and the effects continued to be felt well into the 1980s, arguably exacerbated by Thatcherism, Reaganomics, and the transition to industrial economies in so-called developing or Third World nations. These countries adopted Fordist mass production methods but not its consumption features and therefore offered a low-cost alternative to the higher waged domestic labour market in the West (Schoenberger 1987, 1988). The 'capital flight' and North–South trade that resulted were seen as a cause of deindustrialization in developed countries and of a raft of consequent social problems principally affecting low-skilled workers in industry (Bluestone and Harrison 1982). With the benefit of hindsight, we might argue that the causes and consequences of deindustrialization were and continue to be not purely economic, but socio-economic and connected with the changing nature of production and labour in advanced economies.[1]

A new literature emerged in response to these so-called crises. The disciplinary tributaries of the 1960s and 1970s – sociology, economics, futurology, and management – remained robust. However, a new wave of literature from sociology and, in addition, cultural studies and philosophy, appeared as theorists sought to account for the economic crises of the times and to take into account the synergies of the emergent social and political economies, science and technology, globalization and, increasingly, post-modern culture (Harvey 1989; Jameson 1984; Lyotard 1984). This led to new theorizations of the times, including the concepts of the second industrial divide (Piore and Sabel 1984); disorganized capitalism (Lash and Urry 1987); and New Times (Hall and Jacques 1990). These emerged from the various schools of post-Fordism and sought to explain the emergent trends in production practices and their economic and social impact.

In terms of impact on knowledge economy policies, perhaps the most influential and enduring of the various strands of post-Fordism is the approach which originated in the Science Policy Research Unit (SPRU), University of Sussex, under the auspices of Christopher Freeman. Freeman and his colleagues drew on Schumpeterian evolutionary economics, in particular the notion of innovation as a driver of economic growth, to inform their attempts to theorize the dynamics of technology, growth and trade in the 1980s. Schumpeter's own work on capitalist evolution emphasizes 'innovation as the driving force behind economic, social and institutional change [and] the central role played by capitalist firms in this process' (Fagerberg 2002: 4).

Following Marx, Schumpeter locates the impetus for capitalist evolution in technological competition rather than price competition as traditionally understood and as described by Peters (2003a, 2003b) in his discussion of Hayek. The competition that counts is the 'competition from the new commodity, the new technology, the new source of supply, the new type of organization' (Schumpeter 1943: 84, quoted in Fagerberg 2002: 7).

Innovation facilitates further innovation and is accompanied by a tendency to concentrate or 'cluster' – a phenomenon encouraged by much knowledge economy policy today. Innovation is further defined by its entrepreneurial aspect, and thus occurs within the economic sphere and with a commercial purpose. Indeed, it is not the particular type of innovation which distinguishes a particular epoch, but the commercial processes of the epoch (Schumpeter 1939: 168). By contrast, neo-Schumpeterian Carlota Perez (1983, 1985) draws on the work of Kondratiev to link dominant technologies (key factor industries such as microelectronics) with economic cycles and the resulting techno-economic paradigm, with new ways of organizing economic and, ultimately, social life (Fagerberg 2002: 22). This theorization also stands in contrast to Bell's (1979) view, described above, which attributes social change to new modes of communication rather than communication technologies themselves.

Meanwhile, Freeman, Perez, and others at the SPRU directed their research activity to the notion of national systems of innovation, those 'networks of institutions in the public and private sectors whose activities and interactions initiate, import, modify, and diffuse new technologies' (Freeman 1987: 4). The principles of this and related neo-Schumpeterian research was to influence the development of innovation policy by supranational organizations such as the OECD (1996, 1999a, 1999b, 2001a, 2001b, 2001c) and nation-states, including Australia (Commonwealth of Australia 2001). We elaborate on these themes in Chapter 2.

Conceptual recycling in policy circles in the 1990s

> We are very much talking about the knowledge-based society, but behind that we have the term 'knowledge-based economy' and I think to understand that we have to go back to . . . the Council of Ministers in the OECD in 1994. At that time they decided on an employment strategy . . . to create new knowledge, new skills and to do it in a lifelong learning relation. That was very important and from 1994 we saw more and more publications, discussions and so on about the knowledge-based economy.
>
> (Senior staff member, European Trade Union Committee for Education)

As Morris-Suzuki (1988: 8) says of the term 'information society', all of the terms discussed in this chapter are 'more often used than defined'. This 'comfortable elasticity of definition' does not mean that the concepts are 'vacuous' ones (ibid.). It is perhaps this lack of precision that saw the emergence of competing terms in the 1990s. Theories of the learning society and learning economy, for instance, appeared in the early 1990s and knowledge(-based, -driven) economy and knowledge society reappeared in the mid-1990s. The use of all of these terms has been equally imprecise, although it is arguable that each represents an inflection of a fundamental idea. In the early 1990s, information society and information economy policy, portfolios, and initiatives tended to consolidate around the diffusion of ICTs and ICT skills throughout the economy and society more broadly. Among other things, themes include e-commerce, e-government, e-learning, access and the digital divide, education and information literacy, and information security, rights and ethics.

The 1990s saw the narrow focus on ICTs (and the transmission, storage, and retrieval of information) of the information revolution give way to a growing awareness of the role in the economy of innovation in science and technology more generally. This was associated with an emphasis on the related roles of education and national systems of innovation produced by policy directed towards collaboration between government, academe, and industry. In other words, the focus shifted to the *knowledge base* of economies and societies, the importance of which was anticipated by Drucker in 1969.

Speaking of the United States at that time, Drucker (1969: 356) argues that 'building and maintaining the right knowledge base for intellectual, economic, social, and military performance is essential for national survival'. What is required is 'a knowledge base that encourages everyone to become knowledgeable' (ibid.: 361) and education is clearly central to this. The notion of a 'knowledge-based economy' (Drucker 1993: 168), by contrast, relates to the behaviour of knowledge as an economic resource, which he discusses in the context of the economics of knowledge and the work of the New Growth theorists (see below) and others involving notions of knowledge-based innovation. The major players in this process of disseminating the notion of the knowledge-based economy and society were, and continue to be, supranational organizations, in particular the OECD, the European Union, the World Trade Organization, and the World Bank.

In contrast to the theoretical and speculative literature that emerged in the previous decades, the OECD draws on empirical evidence ('best practice') to describe – and prescribe – the parameters of the knowledge-based economy and associated concepts. With a nod to its conceptual tributaries (Schumpeter, Machlup and Porat, and post-industrialism), the OECD (1996: 9, original emphases) explains that:

> The term '*knowledge-based economy*' results from a fuller recognition of the role of knowledge and technology in economic growth. Knowledge, as embodied in human beings (as '*human capital*') and in technology, has always been central to economic development. But only over the last few years has its relative importance been recognised, just as that importance is growing. The OECD economies are more strongly dependent on the production, distribution, and use of knowledge than ever before.

In this document, the knowledge-based economy functions as the overarching term that encompasses variant and related notions of the information society, network society and learning economy. Hereafter, we call this the knowledge economy discourse or knowledge economy policy. These are generally oriented towards and facilitated by information and communications technology in the global economy. In regard to the information society, for instance,

> It is the increasing codification of some elements of knowledge which have led the current era to be characterised as '*the information society*' – a society where a majority of workers will soon be producing, handling and distributing information or codified knowledge.
>
> (Ibid.: 13, original emphasis)

Thus, while the knowledge economy is related to the information society, it is not simply the information society under a different name. The knowledge economy reappears in policy discourses as part of an evolving conceptual trajectory. Knowledge is a far broader concept than information, which, as we have seen, ultimately comes down to data. Likewise, technology in the knowledge economy includes, but goes well beyond, information technologies. Indeed, it is not a particular technology *per se* that drives the economy.

According to New Growth (Romer 1986) and other endogenous growth theories (Howitt 2000) economic growth is driven by technological progress or innovation that involves the inputs of existing knowledge and human capital to make new and improved knowledge products. Technological change is oriented to market imperatives and technology is equated with knowledge generated through applied or commercial research (OECD 1996). Indeed, it is 'the context of application' that 'describes the total environment in which scientific problems arise, methodologies are developed, outcomes are disseminated and uses are defined' (Nowotny *et al.* 2003: 186).

Endogenous growth theory differs from classical economic theory, which acknowledges the importance of knowledge to economic growth but regards knowledge as exogenous to – that is external to – the economic process or growth model (Solow 1970). In endogenous models of macroeconomic growth, knowledge is considered to be internal to the model, and grows as a result of maximizing the behaviour of knowledge workers and knowledge resources.

This puts knowledge at the centre of economic policies and is what makes investment in human capital via education, training, and funding research and development, so important to economic growth. It is this that helps better explain the significance of policy interventions in knowledge-producing sectors like education and research. Such interventions are designed to encourage, among other things, the:

- creation of research 'clusters' and 'centres of excellence' to assist with the generation of new knowledge and critical mass;
- formation of transdisciplinary and transnational networks to assist with access to the best knowledge;
- promotion of collaborative relationships between educational institutions and firms or industry to help spread risk and resources and to assist with the commercialization of research;
- identification of national research priorities;
- provision of incentives to increase enrolment in the so-called 'enabling' sciences (mathematics, physics, and chemistry) to feed the applied sciences;
- innovation and entrepreneurial activities at all levels of knowledge production;
- acquisition of generic 'employer-friendly' skills, including communication skills, learning ability, problem-solving skills, the ability to work in teams, and self-management;
- development of ICT skills and lifelong learning for all.

All of these measures are designed to maximize knowledge production and thus economic growth. They impact at all levels of work and education, although arguably most acutely in higher education, which plays a key role in national systems of innovation. They also impact on how we understand knowledge and its relation to the economy.

One body of research on knowledge which we alluded to above in the work of David and Foray (2003) identifies the constituents of the knowledge base of an economy and the facilitators of knowledge in terms of tacit and codified knowledge. Lundvall (1998), Lundvall and Archibugi (2001a, 2001b) and Lundvall and Johnson (1994) identify the sub-groupings within this schema. Know-what and know-why can be codified and transferred, traded and quantified as information. Know-who and know-how are tacit (Polanyi 1958, 1966) which means they are complex and variable procedural competencies influenced by experiential and environmental factors. As Lundvall (1998: 9) points out, the advent of information technology and the recognition of its economic potentials have favoured codified knowledge. This, as we have seen, is often seen as synonymous with information. Such favouring of codified knowledge is, in turn, reflected in the focus on the acquisition of ICT skills, regardless of whether the context is the information society, knowledge economy, or knowledge society (see, for example, DEST 2000; European Commission 2002a). The privileging of codified knowledge over tacit knowledge also has implications for certain parts of the knowledge stock. Scientific and technological knowledge are privileged over social science and humanities knowledge because, on the one hand, they are more amenable to codification, and on the other hand, because their 'codification, standardization and normalization' is seen to increase the rate of innovation and so economic growth (see also Chapters 3 and 5).

The concepts of Mode 1 and Mode 2 knowledge production theorized by Gibbons *et al.* (1994) provide a further account of this change with less emphasis on technology and more emphasis on the blurring of knowledge, education, and economy. Clearly most relevant to higher education, it is in this theorization of knowledge production that the principles of the knowledge economy are most transparent. In *The New Production of Knowledge: the dynamics of science and research in contemporary societies*, Gibbons *et al.* distinguish between the cognitive and social practices of Mode 1 (or traditional, specialized academic) knowledge which is exogenous, and Mode 2 (or socially-distributed) knowledge which is endogenous, to the innovation process. Elsewhere, Gibbons (1998: online) summarizes further differences between the two:

> in Mode 1 problems are set and solved in a context governed by the, largely academic, interests of a specific community. By contrast, Mode 2 knowledge is carried out in a context of application. Mode 1 is disciplinary while Mode 2 is transdisciplinary. Mode 1 is characterized by homogeneity, Mode 2 by heterogeneity [it crosses disciplines and institutions, national, and cultural borders]. Organizationally, Mode 1 is hierarchical and tends to preserve its form, while Mode 2 is heterarchical and transient. Each employs a different type of quality control. In comparison with Mode 1, Mode 2 is more socially accountable and reflexive. It includes a wider, more temporary and heterogeneous set of practitioners, collaborating on a problem defined in a specific and localized context.

The shift to issue-based, collaborative, and transdisciplinary research with commercial applications may have initially represented an adaptation or accommodation to the evolving knowledge economy – in particular, the massification of higher education and competition for resources in the post-welfare state. However, taken up by policy-makers (see Kemp 1999; OECD 1996), the notion of Mode 2 knowledge production has become increasingly prescriptive, leading Nowotny *et al.* (2003) to assert that their thesis has been exploited, oversimplified, and opportunistically manipulated by policy-makers. They now argue that it is necessary to think beyond the context of 'application' as the total environment of knowledge production, which they say actually reinforces hierarchical, linear, and positivist approaches. They suggest that what is needed is a capacity 'to reach beyond the knowable context of application to the unknowable context of implication' (ibid.: 192).

From economy to society? The early 2000s

> Whereas the concept of information society is mainly characterized by technological innovation, the concept of knowledge societies includes

> the dimension of social, cultural, economic and political institution transformation.
>
> (Senior staff member, UNESCO, Information Society Division)

The notion of a knowledge society is a highly-contested concept (Webster 1995), as we have indicated, and while increasingly used in policy circles, it is generally under-theorized in respect to social policy development (Trewin 2002). The scholarly literature on the subject is variously utopian – the knowledge society promises 'greater affluence, leisure and intellectual creativity' – and dystopian – it augurs 'profound threats to economic welfare and political freedom' (Morris-Suzuki 1988: 1). Even the most thorough and widely-cited theorization, Bell's (1973) post-industrial thesis, is, in many ways, an exercise in social forecasting. Nonetheless, according to Böhme and Stehr:

> The shift from social forces such as labor or property which were constitutive of industrial society and its social relations, to science and technology or, as Bell describes it, to theoretical knowledge, in the post-industrial society justifies a general reference to these societies as *knowledge societies*.
>
> (1986: 5, original emphases)

Others are more cautious in positing such a shift from a knowledge economy to a knowledge society. Writing in 1969, Drucker stated: 'It may be premature (and certainly would be presumptuous) to call ours a "knowledge society" – so far we only have a knowledge economy' (18). At the beginning of the twenty-first century this is arguably still the case.

There is a tendency in knowledge economy policies to assume that increased economic wealth at a national level will deliver prosperity to all; the so-called 'trickle down' effect. Yet, at the same time as the development and diffusion of knowledge economy policies are intensifying, many social problems remain including such issues as social polarization, friction, and exclusion. While policy-makers at the national, international, and supra-national levels are increasingly using the rhetoric of the knowledge society, the idea of a knowledge society is often reduced to the notion of participation in the knowledge economy or information economy. The European Commission, for instance, uses the term knowledge society in order 'to stress the fact that the most valuable asset is investment in intangible, human and social capital and that the key factors are knowledge and creativity' and, so, in regard to 'new employment possibilities, more fulfilling jobs, new tools for education and training, easier access to public services, increased inclusion of disadvantaged people or region' (European Commission 2003b: online). Here social exclusion is conflated with unemployment and thus exclusion from the knowledge economy. The possibility that the knowledge economy may create the very inequities the knowledge society seeks to resolve is not considered.

This example is symptomatic of a policy tendency to focus on knowledge as a productive force at the expense of an analysis of the way such knowledge 'penetrates and transforms social relations' and 'why and how scientific and technological knowledge comes to acquire its enormous societal relevance and force' (Böhme and Stehr 1986: 5). While the European Community retains a strong social democratic element relative to, say, the USA, Australia, and the UK, and supranational governmental bodies like the OECD and World Bank, the issue of social exclusion, nonetheless, tends to be 'framed residually in terms of trying to address the problems of economic and social polarities without modifying the fundamental tenets of neo-liberalism' (Henry *et al.* 2001: 159). 'Within such a framework,' Henry *et al.* (ibid.: 162) continue, 'exclusion is cast in terms of a failure to engage with the global economy (in turn interpreted largely as a lack of appropriate skills or disposition)'.

There is a further dimension to the limitations of knowledge society discourses in policy circles. This is articulated by the rationale of UNESCO's Education Forum on Higher Education, Research and Knowledge held in December 2003, the theme of which was 'Knowledge Society versus Knowledge Economy: Knowledge, Power and Politics'. According to the Forum website,

> Most debates on change and transformation, irrespective of geographical location, consider the consequences of globalization and the event of the 'knowledge societies'. The major emphasis, however, lies upon knowledge society viewed within the setting of the 'knowledge economy'. This often takes place without a critical view of what the meaning, significance and consequences are that follow the ways in which 'knowledge' itself is currently being re-defined, re-interpreted and applied.
>
> (UNESCO 2003)

Currently knowledge society policies fail to differentiate themselves from knowledge economy policies in a substantial and significant way. As our genealogy suggests, this is in part at least because the knowledge society shares the very same historical and conceptual trajectory as the knowledge economy.

We have shown that since the 1960s, knowledge has been progressively and more intensively redefined along economic lines. Along with the pivotal role of ICT, influential thinking such as Romer's New Growth theory, Freeman's National Systems of Innovation and Gibbon *et al.*'s Mode 2 knowledge has contributed to the privileging of knowledge that can be digitized, commodified, codified, quantified, and applied. Such thinking has had a powerful impact on which knowledge is seen to matter, who has access to it, who controls it and for what purpose. The intensification of the economic function of knowledge has come at the expense of the social function of knowledge. Attention to the social ramifications of understandings of knowledge has tended to come as something of an afterthought to knowledge economy policy. And, of course, in understanding the elevation of the knowledge economy over the knowledge society, we need to bear in mind not only the nature of the knowledge economy, but also the broader character of modern economics.

Modern economics is distinguished by its differentiation from wider society and its tendency to abstract itself from the specificities of time and place, obligation and power, and political, social, and cultural institutions. In his commentary on Polanyi's (1977) analysis, Holton (1992: 18) explains that in modern definitions of the economy, markets

> are not designed to reaffirm social bonds between those who use them. Indeed, it does not matter whether producers or consumers know each other or are members of a common community. Here economic relations are differentiated from wider social concerns rather than embedded within them.

Differentiated economies based on self-regulating markets separate the economy from society. The knowledge economy is, we suggest, a differentiated economy. The fundamentally economic orientation to knowledge it promotes is problematic in a number of ways that we will elaborate in the chapters to follow. Suffice it to say here that they include: the scientization of society and its associated risks, the diminishment of the public sphere, modes of exchange and social bonds that are not market-based, and the commodification of all forms of life including culture and ecology. It is Polanyi's view that the separation between economy and society in differentiated economies cannot be sustained in practice. As Holton (ibid.) goes on to explain, Polanyi believes that 'differentiated market economies generate such extreme social and political tensions that new types of "embedded" economies emerge'; these economies are based on reciprocity, redistribution, or household.

We take a somewhat different approach in this book. We argue that whilst the knowledge economy is predominantly a differentiated economy, it is not uniformly so. Precisely because the economy and society are interrelated, the knowledge economy does, in effect, but not wilfully, provoke the emergence of other economies. In other words, the knowledge economy contains its own contradictions – contradictions it seeks to exclude or marginalize. These contradictions arise, in part, at the limits of the scientization and commodification processes noted above. We postulate the existence of four alternative economies that variously reflect and extend Polanyi's taxonomy and that arise from these processes, and the problems associated with them. These are, as indicated, the risk, gift, libidinal, and survival economies. Each implicitly raises questions about the implications for society of the knowledge economy and points to the problems of the collapsing of economy and society in knowledge economy policies.

* * *

We have suggested that the knowledge economy discourse is haunted by its own contradictions. A central contradiction is between its current sense of certainty and its historical ambiguity. It proffers its views of itself and its future trajectory as solid and certain. Its certainties, we indicated, are about making knowledge the centrepiece of economic policy and about making economics the centrepiece of knowledge policy (research, education, learning). They involve, as we have implied, reductionist views of knowledge and of economics. There is a 'certain' presumption that the social can adequately be addressed, through this reductive formula; indeed that the economic can subsume the social, and that distinctive knowledge about the social and the cultural is not required in the formulation of economic or knowledge policy. However, we have suggested that the apparently solid foundations of the knowledge economy's certainty begin to waver once its proclaimed relationship to the knowledge society is interrogated.

Such certainties also dissolve because the knowledge economy brings to its views of the present and the future a highly ambiguous history: a history it selectively remembers, refuses to recognize, or doesn't even know. Derrida (1994: xix) argues that 'being-with specters' is 'a politics of memory, of inheritance, and of generations'. The ghost of the knowledge economy discourse reminds it that there is a politics to what it remembers and denies of its past. It has become heir to an intellectual tradition that spans many disciplines, and that involves much dispute about such things as trends in production practices, and their actual and likely economic and social impact. It has, however, made clear political choices about what knowledge it has 'inherited'; about the previous generations of thought that it acknowledges and dismisses. Its history is not linear, not a simple 'succession of a before and an after', cause and effect. And thus it cannot claim 'a reassuring order of presents'. Its ghosts will not allow this, for, as Derrida says,

> The spectral moment, [is] a moment that no longer belongs to time, if one understands by this word the linking of modalized presents (past present, actual present: 'now', future present). We are questioning this instant, we are asking ourselves about this instant that is not docile to time, at least to what we call time. Furtive and untimely, the apparition of the specter does not belong to that time ...
>
> (1994: xx)

Note

1 According to a spokesperson for an international trade union organization based in Paris, the changing labour market continues to impact on particular segments of the labour force. He argues that 'if there is anything like an inclusive knowledge-based economy or an information society is to emerge, we are in strong need of

[training] practices which are front-loaded. That is to say, most job-related training is offered to younger employees, is offered to male employees, is offered to already highly or well-skilled, well-trained employees. We need to focus on less-skilled employees, females and on migrants as well' (Senior staff member, Trade Union Advisory Committee).

2 The risk economy

> "Are these the shadows of the things that Will be, or are they the shadows of things that May be, only?"
> Still the Ghost pointed downward to the grave by which it stood.
> "Men's courses will foreshadow certain ends, to which, if persevered in, they must lead," said Scrooge. "But if the courses be departed from, the ends will change. Say it thus with what you show me!"
>
> (Dickens, *A Christmas Carol*, [1843] 2003: 108)

The Ghost of Christmas Future does not show Scrooge what he desires to see. Scrooge wants reassurance that the decision he makes to change the present course of his life will change his future. Such reassurance cannot be given to him. At the appearance of the ghost, past, present and future no longer exist as discrete and consecutive points in time. 'Time,' as Hamlet says, 'is out of joint.' But the temporal ambiguity that the ghost creates does not mean that the future can be known with absolute certainty in advance of the present moment in time. Like The Ghost of Christmas Yet To Be, a silent figure shrouded in black, the future is insubstantial, undisclosed, uncertain. The consequences of Scrooge's present decision are yet to unfold in historical time and cannot be guaranteed. Nonetheless, he has the responsibility to decide. Such responsibility potentially calls into play ethico-political decisions.

The Ghost of Christmas Yet To Be is the 'ghost of the undecidable' (Derrida 1992a: 24), the ghost that haunts the decision. For Derrida the decision is that which is not prescribed or programmed by political or institutional systems or structures. The decision-making process involves a struggle to the extent that the outcome of this process is not a foregone conclusion and its consequences cannot be calculated. A decision once made does not, however, banish the ghost of the undecidable. It remains haunted by the decision not made, by the possibilities rejected, by the course not taken. Most of all, it continues to be haunted by the intransigent unforeseeability of the future. The future is spectral. However, according to Lucy's interpretation, for Derrida 'this doesn't mean that the present and past are wholly calculable, objective, actual, real and the like in contrast to the future's phantasmagoric non-presence. That opposition [comes] undone at the first sign of a ghost' (2004: 116). The future consequences of our past and present decisions are never certain. It is for this reason that uncertainty is seen to involve risk; commonly, but not universally, understood as hazard or danger.

In this chapter, we focus on the ways in which undecidability and risk haunt techno-scientific innovation in the knowledge economy. Techno-scientific innovation is understood as the key driver of economic growth in the knowledge economy. One cannot say for certain that such innovation will bring global economic prosperity, improved health and well-being, ecological sustainability and reduced inequalities. By the same token, one cannot be sure that it will bring economic crises, ecological disaster, pandemics, or widening inequalities. The consequences for present and future generations are undecidable precisely because the future is unforeseeable.

Yet, for Lucy (ibid.: 117),

> This notion of a radically unforeseeable future which remains forever open and to come is precisely what every politics, every political programme, turns a blind eye to. But in turning away from spectrality, in avoiding the question of the being-there of the ghost, every politics is less responsible than it should be to an emancipatory desire for a better world. To avoid the being there of the ghost is to avoid being true to justice.

Knowledge economy policies turn a blind eye to the undecidability of techno-scientific innovation. Instead, they seek to replace uncertainty with certitude. In so doing, they seek to represent the knowledge economy as a project that is 'the reassuring object or the logical or theoretical consequence of assured knowledge (euphoric, without paradox, without aporia, free of contradiction, without undecidabilities to decide)' (Derrida 1998: online). Lucy (2004: 1) explains 'aporia', 'A Greek term denoting a logical contradiction ... is used by Derrida to refer to what he often calls the "blind spots" of any metaphysical discourse'. Risk and undecidability are such blind spots in the knowledge economy.

In the knowledge economy, the economic concept of innovation functions as the 'assured knowledge' which 'programmes' or pre-empts the decision-making of governments, organizations and individuals. As the basis of innovation policy, such assured knowledge means that the knowledge economy is in danger of becoming 'a machine that runs without us, without responsibility, without decision, at bottom without ethics, nor law, nor politics' (Derrida 1998: online). A decision is not a decision if it is programmed or prescribed. As Derrida (ibid.) argues, 'There is no decision or responsibility without the test of aporia or undecidability.' Thus, the illusion of certitude that the economics of innovation creates does not succeed in banishing the ghosts of undecidability and risk.

Despite their claims to programme the future, knowledge economy policies cannot contain the risks (understood as dangers) associated with techno-*scientific* innovation (Bullen *et al.* 2006). And these take many forms. As Ulrich Beck (1992, first published 1986) explains, some such risks are associated with nuclear, chemical, biological, lifestyle and ecological hazards. While this is an important insight, it is our view that risk should not be understood simply as the by-product of scientific hubris. Risk, we will argue, is inherent to the innovation process. It is a specifically techno-*economic* phenomenon involving the economic control and exploitation of scientific and technological undecidability. This logic of control and exploitation is the focus of this chapter.

We begin with a brief discussion of some ways in which sociology and economics discuss the notion of risk. In so doing we offer some theoretical beginnings to a notion of risk economy which draws from the insights of both fields. This is followed by an elaboration of the notion of innovation as it informs and is manifest in knowledge economy policies. We then explain the relationship between a risk economy (as we have tentatively defined it) and innovation, pointing to two things: first its impact on nation-state policy and second the flow-on effects on organizational policy in the techno-scientific industries. Our focus subsequently is on the way innovation policy works to construct its preferred human subject, the technopreneur. We shall argue that the technopreneur is both a subject and agent of innovation policy. It is the technopreneur as agent who invites the ghost of undecidability into the policy machine (a 'machine that runs without us' in Derrida's words). The ghost of undecidability potentially compounds the risk to the future, as we will show. But it also introduces the possibility of the ethico-political decision, an option that the Ghost of Christmas Yet To Be offers Scrooge. We explore this possibility in the final section of this chapter through the idea of responsibility.

Contextualizing risk

So far we have used the term risk unproblematically, relying on commonsense understandings. Yet, the meanings of risk are much debated and highly contextual as Douglas and Wildavsky (1982: 9) explain:

> people who adhere to different forms of social organization are disposed to take (and to avoid) different kinds of risk. ... Questions about acceptable levels of risk can never be answered just by understanding how nature and technology interact. What needs to be explored is how people agree to ignore most of the potential dangers that surround them and interact so as to concentrate only on selected aspects.

It can be inferred from this that risk is not only culturally and historically specific, but also that it is likely to be understood differently by different disciplines. That said, it is not necessarily the case that all disciplines understand risk as a socio-cultural construction. Whereas sociologists tend to, economists tend not to regard risk in this way.

Sociologists of risk are apt to contrast contemporary meanings of risk with historical understandings (see, for example, Beck 1995; Giddens 1999; Lupton 1999). It is commonplace for such sociological accounts to begin with a contrast between pre-modernity and modernity. The key distinction here is that in pre-modernity there was no concept of risk. There were dangers or hazards to be confronted but the misfortunes and accidents of life were believed to be the result of fate, an act of God or the forces of nature. They lay beyond the scope of human control or responsibility. According to Giddens (1999: online), 'Risk refers to hazards that are actively assessed in relation to future possibilities. It only comes into wide usage in a society that is future-oriented.' The concept of risk and its changing meaning, then, is associated with the emergence of modernity, and so the Enlightenment, industrial revolution, and birth of capitalism. As Elliot (2002: 295) says, the notion of risk became 'bound up with the development of instrumental rational control'. This involves the belief that knowledge, in particular scientific knowledge, makes it possible to know, predict and manage hazards and dangers and to statistically predict and economically exploit risk. Furthermore, in modernity, because the calculus of risk promises a means to control the accidental, it is associated with progress.[1] Such views of risk are still common in the discipline of economics as we will explain in more detail shortly. But first let us turn to Beck's concept of risk society as it stands in stark contrast with a notion of risk as amenable to calculation and control.

Modern societies have now reached a historical phase, according to Beck (1994: 5), 'in which the social, political, economic and individual risks increasingly tend to escape the institutions for monitoring and protection'. Techno-scientific innovation has unleashed 'a destruction of the calculus of risk by which modern societies have developed a consensus on progress' (Elliot 2002: 296).[2] The outcome is what Beck calls risk society, in which 'the central problem of western societies is not the production and distribution of "goods" such as wealth and employment ... but the prevention and minimization of "bads"; that is, risks' (Lupton 1999: 59). Beck addresses the implications of this in his theory of reflexive modernization.

In Beck's view, risk society is reflexive in that it is no longer 'blind and deaf' to its 'own effects and threats' (1994: 6). 'Simple modernization', according to Beck, involves the control of nature through the application of science and technology. It is associated with a scientistic culture which in turn controls and legitimates industrial society (Lash and Wynne 1992; Mitchell 1999). Reflexive modernization, by contrast, involves a *confrontation* with the processes and destructive consequences of simple modernization. In particular it recognizes the high consequence risks associated with simple modernity and involves a reflex reaction to the processes that have produced such risks.[3] That is to say, the *lack* of reflection of simple modernity has created the risks that have necessitated subsequent confrontations.

Beck's risk society thesis and more broadly the sociology of risk provides an important analytical resource for this chapter. This is because it focuses on the nexus between risk, knowledge and techno-scientific innovation. However, as we have explained, risk cannot be reduced to the hazards or the incalculable outcomes of techno-science alone. Further, if we are to argue that the knowledge economy is haunted by the risk economy, not the risk society, however unclear this distinction is in Beck's work, we need to think further about the differences between sociological concepts of risk and those from economics. Certainly, Beck acknowledges the complicity of science and capital as a driver of risk creation, but we go further. We support Reddy's argument that 'Mainstream economics may ... constitute the foremost rationalizing discourse and intellectual tool for social justification in our time' (1996: 225). As such, economics imposes itself and its views of risk on social organizations and social actors. This is particularly so in the knowledge cultures of the techno-sciences of the knowledge economy.

In current economic parlance, risk is commonly defined as a situation where there are different possible outcomes that are amenable to probabilistic analysis. Along the Enlightenment lines discussed earlier, such analysis is understood as scientific knowledge. Risk is not seen to include uncertainty because uncertainty cannot be calculated. Indeed, Reddy (ibid.: 222) points to 'The triumph within economics of the notion of "risk" ... or a vision of the future as subject to probabilistic analysis, over "uncertainty".' Uncertainty, he says, is seen to involve 'a vision of the future so fundamentally and radically indeterminate as to preclude such analysis'. It is thus linked with a lack of knowledge or, at best, opinion, and therefore with subjectivity.

One problem associated with the notion of risk (as calculable) in contemporary economics is the illusion of control that it creates. A further and more subtle problem is that 'risk' thus defined omits uncertainty. However, even as it excludes the unpredictable, the unknowable and the subjective, it incorporates them. Of course this delusion of exclusion has not always been the case in economics. Reddy draws on Keynes (1937) to argue that uncertainty is fundamental to the economy, specifically in relation to the behaviour of the human actors involved, be they consumers, entrepreneurs or investors. Keynes, he argues, 'fully rejected attempts to systematically know the future or individuals' ... perceptions of [the future] in terms of rational calculability' on the basis that:

> New fears and hopes will, without warning, take charge of human conduct. All these pretty, polite techniques, made for the well-paneled board room and a nicely regulated market, are liable to collapse. At all times, the vague panic, fears and equally vague and unreasoned hopes are not really lulled and lie but a little way under the surface.
>
> (Keynes 1937, quoted in Reddy 1996: 229)

In her analysis of the changing meanings of risk in economics and other fields, Lupton (1999) observes that the notion that risks can be both good and bad has been lost in contemporary theorizations. Drawing on Short (1984), Lupton (1999: 8) points to the 'short shrift' that good risks receive in technical and bureaucratic assessments of risk. And, drawing on Luhmann (1993), she notes the relative absence of notions of good risks in the current 'esoteric parlance of economic speculation' (Lupton 1999: 8).

It is our view that any adequate notion of a risk economy must at least be able to accommodate the various economic inflections of risk, on the one hand, the will to certainty through probabilistic analysis and associated technologies of control and, on the other hand, the certainty of uncertainty. It also might recognize that risk may involve profits and losses and, more broadly, benefits and hazards. A risk economy thus involves the production, distribution and consumption of 'certainty' and uncertainty, benefits and hazards. But more, a risk economy is also conjured in the *différance*, in Derrida's terms, between calculable risk and radical uncertainty, knowledge and unawareness, system and subjectivity.

Derrida's notion of *différance* is a play on the idea of difference upon which the integrity of concepts like truth and identity depend (see also Chapter 4). *Différance*, as Lucy (2004: 27) explains, 'is suppressed in the metaphysical idea of difference'. Difference is assumed to be a source of meaning – the idea being that a thing can be in part defined by what it is not, its difference from other things. *Différance*, by contrast, refers to the traces of the other, of things it is not. In other words, the relation of difference between calculability and unpredictability is actually one of interdependency and what holds them apart is the spatial and temporal spacing of *différance*. Thus,

> Differance marks the opening of a system of differences in which everything acquires meaning and value ... '[W]ithout differance as temporalization, without the nonpresence of the other inscribed within the sense of the present' [Derrida 1976: 71], nothing could be said to have meaning or value in 'itself'.
>
> (Lucy 2004: 27)

In order to show how the knowledge economy is haunted by different inflections of the risk economy (as we have loosely defined it), we turn to the economic thinking that functions as the 'assured knowledge' which programmes innovation policy decisions. Such thinking, according to Beck (1992: 157), 'throws the door open to a feudalization of scientific knowledge practice through economic and political interests and new dogmas'. Indeed, we suggest that the aporia (contradiction or blind spot) in which the spectre of the risk economy is to be found is in narrow economic understandings of risk and their translation into innovation policy.

Programmed innovation

> Some better mind than mine must have somewhere in some back room thought of the possible unintended consequences or the risks associated with [innovation policy]. But these things can become very, very strong government – they become almost dogmas and they get repeated over and over like mantras. There has not been a lot of reflective stuff, you know, real genuine reflection – a bit at the [Innovation] Summit, perhaps, but even that was such a feel-good festival.
>
> (Staff member, Innovation Policy Branch, Department of Industry, Tourism and Resources [Australian Commonwealth Government])

The term innovation is ubiquitous in contemporary policy and managerial discourse. One may thus be inclined to dismiss it as an empty signifier or an instance of managerial speak (Watson 2003). In the context of the knowledge economy, however, innovation denotes a complex of attributes and processes that extend far beyond the creation of something new. An innovation policy background document published on the European Commission's Community Research and Development Information Service (CORDIS) website points to some of the features of innovation when it states that economic

> Competitiveness depends to a far larger extent today than in the past on the ability of manufacturing and service sectors to meet fast-changing market needs as quickly and efficiently as possible through the application of new technology. This capacity to assimilate and apply new knowledge in order to improve productivity and create new products and services relies on scientific inventiveness and entrepreneurial flair. But it is also affected fundamentally by the conditions which permit, encourage and sustain innovative creativity and investment, or those which impede or limit it. In the 21st century, while innovation will be the primary driver of successful industrial and enterprise policy, it must also inform policy in areas such as education, employment law and taxation.
>
> (CORDIS 2002: 2)

This policy statement suggests that key elements of innovation include new knowledge, scientific inventiveness, technology, markets, enterprise, competitiveness and entrepreneurialism.[4] Innovation, therefore, means much more than a new idea or invention or even new knowledge alone. As Fagerberg (2002: 9) puts it, innovation is 'a specific social activity (function) carried out in the economic sphere with a commercial purpose'.

Economist Joseph Schumpeter, who we introduced in Chapter 1, captures the economic importance of innovation when he says, 'The capitalist engine' is kept 'in motion' by the 'new consumers' goods, the new methods of production or transportation, the new markets, the new forms of industrial organization that capitalist enterprise creates' (1943: 83). According to Freeman *et al.* (1982: 19), Schumpeter regarded innovation as a driver of economic growth because new opportunities for profit

> attracted a 'swarm' of imitators and improvers to exploit the new opening with a wave of new investment, generating boom conditions. The competitive processes set in motion by this 'swarming' then gradually eroded the margins of innovative profits (as in Marx's model), but before the system could settle into an equilibrium condition the whole process would start again through the destabilizing effects of a new wave of innovation.

This is associated with the process Schumpeter famously describes as 'creative destruction'. Linked with technical innovation and long wave business cycles, this refers to the 'process of industrial mutation ... that incessantly revolutionizes the economic structure *from within*, incessantly destroying the old one, incessantly creating a new one' (Schumpeter 1943: 83, original emphases).

The evolution of the knowledge economy has been accompanied by a parallel revival of interest in Joseph Schumpeter's economic theory and evolutionary economics more generally. The work of the neo-Schumpeterian school of post-Fordism at the University of Sussex (see, for example, Freeman 1987; Freeman *et al.* 1982; Freeman and Perez 1988) has been particularly influential, most significantly in regard to the link between organizational change, technological innovation and economic development, the so-called techno-economic paradigm theorized by Carlota Perez, a visiting fellow at SPRU, University of Sussex in 1983–4.

Perez's hypothesis is based on Schumpeter's innovation thesis. Like him, she draws on Nikolai Kondratiev's work in the 1920s on 50-year long waves of 'boom' and 'bust' in the development of capitalist economies. These long waves are also referred to as Kondratievs and we can explain their significance by contrasting current and previous business cycles. The fourth Kondratiev was Fordist. Typified by mass production and consumption, its dominant factor industry was electro-mechanical technology. In the current post-Fordist fifth Kondratiev, the major factor industry is microelectronics and the 'key "carrier" sectors' include computers and software, telecoms, computer integrated manufacturing/new materials, information technology (IT) services, biotechnology, space/satellite and environmental technologies (Perez 1985). It is this emphasis on technological innovation as a driver of economic growth which underpins the emphasis on techno-scientific knowledge in the knowledge economy.

Perez (1983: 358) departs from Schumpeter in arguing that business cycles 'are not a strictly economic phenomenon, but rather the manifestation, measurable in economic terms, of the harmonious or disharmonious behaviour of the *total* socio-economic and institutional systems (on the national and international scale)' (original emphasis). The techno-economic paradigm refers to the characteristic modes of economic *and* social change which emerge during a business cycle in response to the technical innovation (or dominant 'factor' industry) which characterizes it. This connection with organizational and institutional cultural change helps to explain the institutionalization of innovation in national systems of innovation (Freeman and Louçã 2001). As the OECD (1996: 7) explains, 'The configuration of national innovation systems, which consist of the flows and relationships among industry, government and academia in the development of science and technology, is an important economic determinant.' Later in this chapter, we look more closely at the impact of national systems of innovation on the organizational level. For now, we consider some of the broader risk implications of innovation thus defined.

The intrinsic risk implications

The first risk implication is associated with the compression of time. Although both Schumpeter's and Perez's notions of innovation are mapped onto Kondratiev's theory of 50-year business cycles, the principles upon which national systems of innovation are based arguably disrupt this time frame. Innovation has become an orchestrated process whereby 'The "coupling" between science, technology, innovative investment and the market, once loose and subject to long time delays, is now much more intimate and continuous' (Freeman *et al.* 1982: 41). In other words, the length of time it takes to generate, develop and commercialize new knowledge has contracted. The innovation process is further accelerated by the global scale of innovation activity and the application of existing technical knowledge. According to the UK White Paper, *Excellence and Opportunity: a science and innovation policy for the 21st century* (Department of Trade and Industry (UK) 2000: online):

> We are doing more research, more productively than previous generations. The dramatic changes that took place at the beginning of the 20th century, such as radio, aviation and mass production, are matched by those of the 21st. What has changed is the scale, and the fact that the new technologies affect everyone, across the globe. Scientific research has been made vastly more productive by information technology which, for example, allows biotechnology researchers to scan thousands of compounds in the time it took a researcher three decades ago to survey a handful.
>
> For Britain to prosper in the 21st century and to be able to play a leading role in the creation of the new global industries, we must have a first class process for pursuing scientific advance and using it successfully. We must have the ability to generate, harness and exploit the creative power of modern science.

As the pace of creative destruction increases, so too, we suggest, does the risk of destructive creation.

Ideologies of linear development and progress constitute a second risk implication. Innovation theory originates in evolutionary economics and therefore supposes an evolutionary trajectory. This resonates with ideologies of progress. It is Beck's (1996) view that belief in progress, one of the sources of meaning of industrial society, has been exhausted and lost the enchantment it once had. Rather than providing the solution to problems, science is increasingly seen as the source. Science's authority, he argues, is undermined by competing and contradictory expert systems. Yet it is precisely a belief in progress that provides the vigour with which governments are embracing notions of the knowledge economy. Certainly there is a widespread assumption that innovation is 'the route to commercial success and prosperity for all' (Blair 1998) and there is a strong future orientation to innovation policy rhetoric (see, for example, Commonwealth of Australia 2001; Department of Trade and Industry (UK) 2000; Government of Canada 2002). This implies a 'developmental trajectory' whereby revolutionary technological innovation is assumed to bring sharp increases in industrial productivity and, with them, prosperity.

As a result, the economic well-being of nation-states is seen to be increasingly dependent on their innovative capacity. Innovation, it seems, does not merely involve a swarm of business imitators driven by new opportunities for profit, as Schumpeter suggested. This swarming occurs at the level of the nation-state, and is driven by the allure of technology's economic promise and by the fear of being squeezed out of an increasingly competitive global marketplace. In this context, risk tends not to be viewed in terms of the unforeseen outcomes of techno-science or the fallibility of economists and scientists alike. Rather, risk is reframed as the consequence of *not* embracing techno-scientific progress. Thus, according to an Australian Commonwealth Government staff member from the National Office of the Information Economy (NOIE), 'The knowledge economy is not a manageable risk in the sense that we don't have the option of saying, "Well, we won't go down the knowledge economy route. I mean, that's a road to serfdom, if you like".'

A third risk implication involves the techno-deterministic view of society that drives knowledge economy thinking. The correlation that is constantly drawn between economic prosperity and scientific advancement points to the view that technology shapes society. As we have explained elsewhere (Bullen *et al.* 2004b) the techno-economic paradigm has been widely criticized as technologically deterministic (see, for example, May 2002; Webster 1995). Such approaches to social change, it is argued, tend to stress 'the independence of technology from social forces' and focus on the 'logical development of one innovation to the next' (May 2002: 26). Technological innovation is implicitly represented as a force over which we have no control, thus inviting passive accommodation of technologically-induced change. Something of the sense of this inevitability is reproduced in *Shaping Australia's Future* when it describes the organizational and economic changes which occur during each long wave and concludes: 'Just as these changes have occurred in the past, they are strongly evident in the current "ICT wave"' (Department of Industry, Science and Resources (ISR) 1999: 10). As such, the changes enumerated in this policy background document do not simply locate the current ICT wave within an historical trajectory. The document is not only descriptive, but prescriptive, representing the past as a guarantor of the future and the techno-economic paradigm as the theoretical knowledge upon which to base innovation policy decisions.

The upshot of all of this is that national innovation policies are steering research and development toward the narrow field of high-risk frontier technologies seen to characterize the fifth Kondratiev (see, for example, Commonwealth of Australia 2001; European Commission 2002b). In so doing, they also promote the development of new social, institutional and market modes, the guidelines for which are set by 'the initial diffusion' of new technological innovations (Perez 1983: 358). This creates disequilibrium and 'provokes the crisis of the old mode' (ibid.), making the restoration of equilibrium contingent on restructuring the outmoded socio-institutional framework in ways that complement the new technological style. Such logic opens the way for policy-makers to dismiss the unanticipated social consequences of a new business cycle as an unfortunate but inevitable side-effect of progress. Thus, in its assessment of the impact of technologization, globalization, and organizational change accompanying the emergence of the knowledge-based economy, the OECD (1996: 18) concludes that 'While there are dislocations in the labour market in the short term, enlightened approaches to knowledge accumulation and learning *should* lead to enhanced growth and job creation in the longer term' (emphasis added).

In the face of such uncertainty, moreover, the process of creative destruction has the effect of committing us on a course to an unknown destination. According to Elam (1994: 45), 'As a critical stage of advancement is reached, it becomes very difficult for national economies and individual firms to opt out of the new technological regime.' Vested interests, if not economic sustainability itself, make it difficult to adequately respond to the unintended effects of technology once new infrastructure is in place. The economic reasoning informing the on-going resistance of the US Bush administration to the Kyoto Protocol on the reduction of greenhouse gases is a case in point.

Of course, technology 'opens a door; it does not compel one to enter' (White 1978: 28). The degree to which innovation becomes autonomous rests on the decisions of governments, institutions and individuals, and the extent to which they perceive a choice to 'enter' or not and their motives for doing so. While it is arguable therefore that the techno-economic paradigm is techno-deterministic, it is more accurate to say, as does Perez, that 'the profit motive is the propeller [while] the technological style is the steering mechanism' (1983: 366) and the final form this style will take 'ultimately depend[s] on the interests, actions, lucidity and relative strength of the social forces at play' (ibid.: 360). This, however, does not prevent the possibility of purposeful action based on the characteristics of the emerging technological style, as in the Australian policy example above. This has also been the net effect of *The Knowledge-based Economy* (OECD 1996). When the OECD described the harmonization of the total socio-economic and institutional systems manifest in the *emergent* knowledge economy, it provided the manifesto and impetus for the creation of national systems of innovation.

National systems of innovation bring the economic, technological and socio-institutional spheres into an unprecedented alliance. Indeed, they become integrated. In this regard, risk is no longer simply a result of the limitations of techno-scientific knowledge, that is, the inadvertent creation of hazards which are 'systemically grounded in the institutional and methodological approach of the sciences to risk' (Beck 1992: 59). Rather, the spectre of risk arises in the very process of the economization of science; in the ways in which the institutional and methodological approaches of economics to risk and uncertainty increasingly inform the creation and application of new scientific knowledge. We now focus on the relationship between these new socio-institutional mechanisms, the subjectivities they seek to shape, and the risk they invoke and provoke.

The ambiguous figure of the technopreneur

> I think what we've really got to instil in people is risk-taking. Not to be risk-averse. Not to be stupid, but to take risks, but risk in a calculated way. You look at the developments in gene technologies and then putting aside the emotive moral argument that there is, you should never stifle the science and creativity side of things. You should always let them explore the possibility – within ethical boundaries – because you may just happen to find that one development could lead to disease mitigation or disease control and that will give you social return in terms of quality of life issues.
>
> (Staff member, International relations and collaboration branch, Department of Education, Science and Training [Australian Commonwealth Government])

Entrepreneurialism is central to the knowledge economy. In this section we consider the role of the entrepreneur, the manner in which it has been bureaucratized and individualized, and particular meanings of risk associated with it. According to Knight,

> The only 'risk' which leads to profit is a unique uncertainty resulting from an exercise of ultimate responsibility, which in its very nature cannot be insured nor capitalized nor salaried. Profit arises out of the

> inherent, absolute unpredictability of things, out of the sheer brute fact that the results of human activity cannot be anticipated and then only in so far as even a probability calculation in regard to them is impossible and meaningless.
>
> (Knight 1921: III.X.33)

In Knight's view, the burden of this uncertainty is ultimately borne by the entrepreneur, the human agent of the innovation process and therefore of economic growth.

The entrepreneur is crucial to the innovation process in that he or she performs the 'combinatory' activity, an activity involving new combinations of existing resources which typifies the 'entrepreneurial function' (Schumpeter [1934] 1978: 84). Schumpeter distinguishes the human agent of innovation from the inventor when he claims:

> As long as they are not carried out into practice, inventions are economically irrelevant. And to carry any improvement into effect is a task entirely different from the inventing of it, and a task, moreover, requiring different kinds of aptitudes. Although entrepreneurs *may* of course be inventors just as they may be capitalists, they are inventors not by nature of their function but by coincidence and vice versa.
>
> (Ibid.: 88–9, original emphasis)

It is 'The ability and initiative of entrepreneurs (who might or might not themselves be inventors but more usually would not be)' (Freeman *et al.* 1982: 19) that, according to this view, creates the opportunities for profits which generate economic growth. More recently, Kirzner (1984: online) has described the entrepreneur as 'the agent that spurs society to take advantage of existing scattered and dispersed knowledge' and who 'generates and harnesses new technological knowledge, and discovers entirely new bodies of resources that had been hitherto overlooked'.

In the knowledge economy there are three significant developments in the conception of the entrepreneurial function in innovation. First – and in this regard Schumpeter (1943) was prescient – innovation is endogenized, although this does not lead to the obsolescence of the entrepreneurial function as he anticipated. The endogenization of innovation implies that with the incorporation of research and development within firms and with collaboration between research institutions and industry, the importance of the individual entrepreneur is increasingly 'superseded by a "bureaucratized" type of innovation' (Freeman *et al.* 1982: 41). As a consequence, the combinatory function of the individual entrepreneur becomes an organizational or social process based on 'knowledge networks' whereby 'interactive learning involving producers and users in experimentation and exchange of information is the driver of innovation' (OECD 1996: 14). One outcome of this is that the innovation process is no longer linear. It does not necessarily begin with new research – typically scientific – and pass sequentially through the various stages of development, production, marketing, and ultimately the consumption of new products. Instead, 'innovation can stem from many sources' and thus 'requires considerable communication among different actors – firms, laboratories, academic institutions and consumers – as well as feedback between science, engineering, product development, manufacturing and marketing' (ibid.). National systems of innovation operate to facilitate this process, with the result that the boundaries between the production of new technology and its commercialization are blurred.

A second development in the notion of the entrepreneurial function is its association with the frontier sciences. Our earlier discussion of the techno-economic paradigm and the fifth Kondratiev points to this increasing policy impetus. The entrepreneur is likewise more and more involved not simply with the creation of new products and new markets, but with new scientific knowledge.

Third, and as a consequence, the functional difference between the agent of innovation and invention no longer holds. Whereas the entrepreneur might not necessarily be an 'inventor' or scientist, in the knowledge economy he or she is likely to be. Thus, in the knowledge economy the entrepreneur is not a purely economic entity. Rather, he or she is a *technopreneurial* subject (Kenway *et al.* 2004a) in whom techno-scientific knowledge and business acumen is combined. S/he is an individual for whom 'being able to draft a business plan should be as natural as doing a scientific experiment or writing a theoretical article' (European Commission 2000: 3). In constructing knowledge as mainly techno-scientific knowledge, innovation policies construct the ideal knowledge worker as a techno-scientist. Further, in constructing knowledge as a commodity rather than a public good, innovation policies construct the ideal knowledge worker as an entrepreneur. In systematizing innovation, innovation policies construct the ideal knowledge worker as a networker, be that social, communicational or informational. In the knowledge economy, the human actor in the innovation process and ideal knowledge worker combines all these functions to become the technopreneur. This hybrid figure both intensifies and disrupts classical understandings of the entrepreneurial function and, in so doing, arguably exceeds the capacity of either economics or science to treat risk as a probability calculation.

One reason why this is so is evident in Spicer and Jones' (2004) discussion of the relationship between the individual entrepreneur and bureaucratized entrepreneurialism or enterprise culture. They challenge the perception of the entrepreneur as a subject driven by economic calculation and point to a fundamental incompatibility between the entrepreneur and enterprise culture (see also du Gay 2004; Fournier and Grey 1999). Spicer and Jones (2004: online) argue that 'real' entrepreneurs do not conform to the image of 'rational calculating machines trawling the seas of financial capital'. On the contrary, they say, entrepreneurs are 'unruly' and 'elusive'; 'embark on schemes of which they could not rationally predict the outcome'; and 'In undertaking such risky adventures they exercise not only their rational faculties and accounting skills, but also act on passions, hunches and mystical visions' (ibid.). As this suggests, the entrepreneurial function is not intrinsically rational and, in line with Knight (1921), is associated with uncertainty rather than calculable risk. Moreover, the entrepreneur is represented as a unique individual, leading Spicer and Jones to conclude that attempts to institutionalize entrepreneurialism as enterprise are nothing but a wasteful folly.

That said, we think that Spicer and Jones underestimate the impact of socio-institutional change (Perez 1983) accompanying innovation – the context in which new subjectivities and new modes of 'risk selection and risk perception' (Douglas and Wildavsky 1982: 9) are emerging. They also assume that the entrepreneur is an economic rather than techno-economic entity and therefore overlook the fact that the institutionalization of technopreneurialism in national systems of innovation is also a potentially hazardous folly. Insofar as supranational and national innovation policies act to steer techno-economic progress 'at a distance', they seek to 'simulate conditions in which employees of large organizations are made to take on the risks and responsibilities' (du Gay 2004: 42) of the innovation process.

Incubating risk in the contemporary university

The impact of these developments is nowhere more evident than in academic research where the imperative to achieve immediately measurable (commercial) impact and competitive advantage stands in stark contrast to the mission of the traditional university (Kenway and Langmead 2002). National and international governance structures are increasingly overseeing the direction of basic and applied research via research priorities, funding guidelines, and incentives to link with industry partners. In response, universities are expanding existing enterprise arms and establishing new ones with the aim of promoting and capturing the commercial potential of the new knowledge they generate. We interviewed staff in the commercialization sections of two Australian universities who take responsibility for the identification and protection of intellectual property, new business incubation and the commercialization of research, which 'involves transferring technology from the inventor's mind to the marketplace in order to generate commercial returns for the inventor and commercial investors' (Research and Innovation section, Australian university).

These interviews revealed a significant difference between these recent initiatives and traditional university enterprises: commercialization is *prospective* rather than *retrospective* in relation to the new knowledge generated by research (Staff members, Research and Innovation section, Australian university). In other words, intellectual property and commercial potential is now considered at the commencement of research in order for the university and/or the technopreneur to retain their monopoly over the new knowledge. In the past, commercial application would have been considered later or at the end of the research process. In the current competitive environment, this is considered to be too late (Staff members, Research and Innovation section, Australian university). What is going on here is not just a matter of protecting intellectual property, but a form of financial speculation. Indeed, it is a form of knowledge speculation for the purposes of profit. As Brown and Michael (2003: 5) explain,

> The more acute the competition, the more urgent is the requirement to push the horizon of competitive action into the future, beyond the gaze of one's competitors. ... An overwhelmed economic environment forces the time horizon of rivalry further and further into the speculative future.

They go on to point out, 'Far from reducing uncertainty, this intensifying engagement with the future leads to a shared escalation of uncertainty' (ibid.: 6).

This uncertainty is highly ambivalent. It is not the same as the economic understanding of risk since, as we have seen, the uncertainty of the innovation process and the potential to profit from it lies in the fact that it is novel, emergent and yet to be. There is no guarantee of profit or economic growth in this scenario because it necessarily remains in the unforeseeable future. Nevertheless, this is part of the allure of innovation, since there is no guarantee of loss either and the possible ill-effects are equally indeterminable and therefore beyond risk calculation.

Uncertainties, as Knight (1921) observes, tend to be converted into economic notions of risk in organized activity. Our interview data from the Research and Innovation section supports this view. Entrepreneurial activity involves financial and market risks for the university, and personal and professional risks (dangers) for the technopreneur, risks which not every academic is willing to take. '[N]ot everybody wants to be a risk-taker at the expectation of a high return' (Staff member, Entrepreneurial section, Australian university), and the 'high return' for many academics might mean no more than establishing or advancing their career, enhancing their professional standing or simply gaining the right to pursue research since access to research funding, whether public or private, is increasingly contingent on fulfilling innovation criteria. Yet even such modest stakes create pressure to produce results, to provide a return on investments and to beat competitors to the market.

Getting in at the 'front end' (Staff members, Research and Innovation section, Australian university) of the innovation process not only fetishizes the new as Brown and Michael (2003) argue. It fetishizes 'the soon to be and a corresponding adjustment to the exploitation of emerging or future opportunities rather than established routines and habits ... Success depends on shortening time frames and, if possible, projecting them into the future' (ibid.: 6). The competitive environment associated with innovation policy, then, has the effect of compressing time and producing a sense of urgency. It has resulted in cases of intellectual theft, less than rigorous scholarship, and a reluctance to engage in the informal and free exchange of ideas as a result of the imperative to publish research findings (Pearson 2004). We discuss some of the associated consequences of this in Chapter 3. In the present context, the goal of innovation is no longer the broader benefits it might bring, but the scientific 'breakthrough' itself. Such circumstances invite the possibility of under-acknowledging or overlooking potential risks (understood as dangers) in the long term. They are subject to the inherent unpredictability of human conduct (Keynes 1937).

This conflicts with the best principles of the academy as well. The drive to commercialize competes with the pressure to publish, but ultimately it creates a comparable compression of time. The technopreneur is advised not to publish until intellectual property is assessed and protected (Staff member, Research and Innovation section, Australian university). This conflicts with traditional academic performance models that measure research performance largely by publication output. Julie Wells, Policy and Research Coordinator for the National Tertiary Education Union in Australia, reiterates this point, noting that 'the environment of commercialization ... will often work to quite different time frames. Short-term time frames will often demand confidentiality and secrecy which doesn't enable the academic to publish' (Australian Broadcasting Corporation 2001a: online). As this suggests, what may constitute delay in academic terms in fact conceals a compression of time created by the urgency to convert knowledge into commodity. In Wells' view, 'in this hothouse environment where commercialization is a matter of survival ... the rush to market can actually compromise the process in a number of ways' (ibid.).

For former Macquarie University (New South Wales) environmental microbiologist Mark Guaci, who with his colleague Graham Veece started the company *Biotechnology Frontiers*, such partiality or compromise is perceived rather than actual. However, he adds,

> We think of ideas all the time but immediately now apply a commercial temper to them. Who's going to buy it? How many people are there? How many are we going to sell? How much are we going to charge? How much is it going to cost to make it? All that stuff, the real basic stuff but that's what we apply to it [new knowledge] almost immediately and that means that ... A lot of R&D isn't done. Also the other thing [is] we just can't afford to do everything we'd like. Being innovative now that we're in a commercial world can be difficult unless you clearly identify that we need to maintain that and we're trying but ... it is more difficult.
>
> (Ibid.)

Economic considerations not only determine what type of research is done, but how much. Time is money and rigorous research takes time and money.

The time frame for testing the world's first treatment for the influenza virus was 'eight years of testing on animals and humans to ensure that Relenza . . . works' (CSIRO 2003: online). In fact, the drug is the result of thirty years of research, the commercial potential of which only became apparent in the last ten years (Australian Broadcasting Corporation 2001a: online).

As these examples suggest, the growth of institutional and individual technopreneurialism compresses and disrupts the temporal duration of knowledge creation. This creates a heightened risk (danger) of releasing under-researched technologies onto the market place, but also the potential loss of life-saving research. At this very literal level 'time is out of joint' and it is this 'disjointedness' that exposes the uncertainty that innovation policy exploits. In so doing, it admits the spectre of the risk economy, that is to say, the possibility of unintended consequences and hazardous side-effects. It also admits the ghost of undecidability.

Beck (1999: 78, original emphasis) argues that undecidability is at the crux of the 'ultimate deadlock of risk society'. 'There is no-one,' he says, 'who really knows the global outcome – at the level of positive knowledge, the situation is radically undecidable – but we none the less [*sic*] *have to decide*'. Such undecidability makes innovation

> an obscene gamble, a kind of ironic reversal of predestination: I am held accountable for decisions which I was forced to make without proper knowledge of the situation. The freedom of decision enjoyed by the subject of the risk [economy] is the 'freedom' of someone who is compelled to make decisions without being aware of their consequences.
>
> (Ibid.)

National systems of innovation institutionalize this predicament and also individualize it in the technopreneur. The danger is not just that, as techno-scientist, the technopreneur must make decisions about the application of new technologies without being able to fully predict their long-term consequences and side effects. The danger arises in the opposition of system and subjectivity and in the tension between innovation as a prescriptive economic process constraining human conduct via calculus, and innovation as an act of scientific invention, the outcomes of which cannot be predicted or prescribed. The tension between economic and scientific conceptualizations of risk and the elision of uncertainty have profound implications for the decision-making process and so our responsibility to the future.

In Derridean terms, however, the ghost of the undecidable introduces the possibility of a different view of uncertainty. As we explained at the beginning of this chapter, a true decision arises in the absence of a preordained or prescribed choice. This is also true of responsibility, since we take no responsibility when a decision is prescribed for us. According to Lucy (2004: 107), 'what Derrida means by responsibility ... involves having to come to terms with the undecidability of differences between and within prescribed and personal decisions'. Given the fact that we must make decisions in the face of a radically indeterminate future, the only true decision is the ethico-political decision. Indeed, Derrida (1992b: 41) ventures so far as 'to say that ethics, politics and responsibility, *if there are any*, will only ever have begun with the experience and experiment of the aporia' (original emphases). It is to such an experiment that we now turn, beginning by contextualizing our discussion in relation to the ethico-political, taking Beck as our starting point.

The risk economy and the ethico-political decision

In risk society, according to Beck, reflexive modernization has both exposed the fallibility of science and given rise to greater lay knowledge of science. Scientific knowledge is no longer the monopoly of the elite. He claims that:

> As scientization proceeds, the systematically produced uncertainty spreads to external relations, and conversely turns the target groups and appliers of scientific results in politics, business and the public into *active coproducers* in the social process of knowledge definition. ... For the target groups and appliers of science, reflexive scientization thus opens up *new possibilities of influence and development* in the processes and production of scientific results. ... It contains the opportunity to emancipate social practice *from* science *through* science.
>
> (1992: 157, original emphases)

As Tulloch and Lupton (2003: 5) explain, 'debate [about risk] is reconstituted in the public sphere in place of modernity's silent collusion of science and capital', suggesting that reflexive modernization is also 'a theory of resistance'. Reflexive modernization results in the demystification and de-monopolization of science and politics, meaning that lay people have greater knowledge of science and are politicized in regard to the risk. We do not dispute this trend, but note a parallel and contradictory trajectory that emerges from innovation policy and which militates against the possibility of the ethico-political decision.

In contrast to industrial society, in which assumptions about the nexus between knowledge and progress depended on the mystification of science, governments globally are implementing national science and innovation awareness campaigns (Fahey *et al.* 2005). One premise here is that a better educated public will be less likely to overestimate the risks and underestimate the benefits of techno-scientific innovation. A more knowledgeable public will be less likely to resist the ideology of scientization. Governments are increasingly engaged not in risk management so much as risk *image* management.

The discussion of public attitudes to science in the knowledge economy in the European Commission's (1995) White Paper on teaching and learning indicates the nature of the problem such resistance presents. In this document, risk society is regarded more as an impediment to, rather than a consequence of, the growth of the knowledge economy. Lay understandings of risk are seen as valid only to the degree to which they conform to objective scientific facts or expert opinion. The corollary of this is a tendency to construct a deficit model of public or lay knowledges (Irwin and Wynne 1996), which are positioned as irrational or subjective. This particular policy document identifies a *fin de siècle* anxiety exacerbated by the media. It represents this anxiety as irrational, noting that 'Instead of celebrating progress as was the case a century ago, public opinion often perceives scientific ventures and technological progress as a threat' (European Commission 1995: 8). It argues that a broad knowledge base across the disciplines is required if Europe is to overcome this anxiety and to cultivate a culture of innovation: 'By demonstrating the link between science and the progress of mankind, while being fully aware of its limitations, today's scientific and technological world will be accepted and in a better position to spread widely an innovative culture' (ibid.).

Risk perception, of course, tends to be culturally specific. Thus, for example, the European Commission currently opposes genetically modified foods but embraces stem cell research. The reverse holds true in the United States where the Bush Administration opposes embryonic stem cell testing. In November 2004, however, Californians voted to support Proposition 71 – the establishment of a new state medical research institute and $3 billion in state funding for stem cell research and research facilities in their state. It was 'a belief in medical research and its ability to find treatments for disease' (Knight 2004: online) which drove the 'yes' vote for Proposition 71. This result belies the loss of faith in expert systems which Beck argues accompanies reflexive modernization. In a rebuttal to the argument that Proposition 71 constituted corporate welfare and bad medicine, the California Attorney General's (2004: 73) report noted that '71 is endorsed by over 20 Nobel Prize winning scientists, medical groups representing 35,000 California doctors and non-profit disease groups representing millions of suffering patients'. The majority of the 40.9 per cent of 'no' votes were attributed not to beliefs about the uncertainties of biotechnology, but risks to the economy (Knight 2004: online). Arguments against Proposition 71 in the Attorney General's report mobilized economic and ethical arguments relating to the use of embryonic stem cells although not stem cell research *per se*. The scientific undecidability of such research remained only as an aporia or blind spot.

As such, the aporia from which the ghost of undecidability emerges potentially compounds the risk to the future. However, it also introduces the possibility of the ethico-political decision in relation to techno-scientific research and therefore responsibility for the future. What might this mean? To explain this, we take as a cameo study a biotechnological research project conducted by SymbioticA in the Department of Anatomy and Human

Biology at the University of Western Australia. The project we describe was precipitated by an inquiry into the future interaction between biotechnologies and industrial design. In the current research, semi-living tissues are constructed by sowing living cells on 3D scaffolds formed out of biodegradable or bio-absorbable polymers, glass, hydrogels (for example, collagen), and surgical sutures. The structures are immersed in nutrient-rich media and incubated and grown in a bio-reactor. The bio-reactor simulates the natural cellular environment, but in the absence of an organic capillary system the capacity to produce large scale formations remains elusive and, therefore, one of the goals of biotechnology, the production of human organs for transplant.

However, this is not the goal of Oron Catts, Ionat Zurr, and their colleagues and postgraduate students at SymbioticA. In fact, SymbioticA is not a science research programme – though it involves tissue engineering – nor is it conducted by scientists. SymbioticA is an art studio, not a laboratory. Initiated in 1996 by Catts, the aim of the Tissue Culture & Art Project (TC&A) is to 'explore questions arising from the use of living tissue to create/grow semi-living objects/sculptures and to research the technologies involved in such a task' (Catts and Zurr 2002: 365). In so doing, it also calls into question new knowledge and raises debate about the direction of biotechnology specifically and the techno-sciences more generally.

Intentionally contentious and culturally and ethically ambiguous, the ambivalence that tissue culture art provokes in the viewer is designed to draw attention to 'our lack of cultural understanding in dealing with new knowledge and control over nature' (ibid.: 370). It is Catts' (2002: online) view that 'As biological research departments in universities are encouraged by governments to partner with "industry" and "defence", the need for research into non-utilitarian purposes become urgent.' For, as he explains,

> Developments in technology are actualized possibilities, not necessarily the only ways knowledge can be utilized ... The exploration of contestable possibilities is important to the understanding of the ways technology may develop. By fostering artistic critical engagements with biological research, SymbioticA provides a 'greenhouse' for developing alternatives to the commercial mainstream.
>
> (Ibid.)

Because they are techno-artists and not techno-scientists, they are differently situated in relation to the hazards of techno-economic progress, which Beck (1992: 59) says are 'systemically grounded in the institutional and methodological approach of the sciences to risk'. In fact when interviewed Catts said,

> I still have a lot of gaps in my understanding of biology, but we, on the other hand, are able to propose things that the scientists would never think about. Sometimes ignorance is bliss, in the sense [that] you're not as programmed to the dogma.

Because they are techno-artists and not technopreneurs, they are not enslaved by the market. This does not mean that commercially viable innovations have not resulted from their research, but that the artists consciously reject the economic as the rationale of their research. In fact, they are trying to achieve the opposite, being openly critical of technopreneurial researchers 'who also own shares in companies which are commercializing the outcome or their own research' (ibid.). The rationale of the TC&A projects is ethico-political, evolving in the context of an awareness of the way the risks of techno-economic progress are compounded by a global climate of terror. As Zurr and Catts (2003: online) explain, 'When the manipulation of life takes place in an atmosphere of conflict and profit driven competition, the long-term results might be disquieting.'

In fact, the anxieties created by the risks of techno-scientific innovation formed the theme of the first gallery exhibition of an art object constructed from living tissue, *Tissue Culture and Art(ificial) Womb 2000*, presented at the Ars Electronica Festival in Linz, Austria. Also entitled *The Process of Giving Birth to Semi-Living Worry Dolls*, the exhibit consisted of seven semi-living versions of Guatemalan worry dolls 'grown' in an artificial womb – the bio-reactor. The dolls were given alphabetical names that represented the artists' worries:

> Doll A: stands for the worry about Absolute Truths and people who think they hold them.
> Doll B: represents the worry of Biotechnology and the forces that drive it (see Doll C).
> Doll C: stands for Capitalism, Corporations.
> Doll D: stands for Demagogy and possible Destruction.
> Doll E: stands for Eugenics and the people who think that they are superior enough to practice it.
> Doll F: the fear of Fear itself.
> Doll G: not a discrete doll, as Genes are present in all semi-living dolls.
> Doll H: symbolizes our fear of Hope.
>
> (Catts and Zurr 2002: 368)[5]

For Zurr and Catts (2003: online) risk inheres in the interaction of ideology and knowledge since 'The form and application of our newly acquired knowledge will be determined by the prevailing ideologies that develop and control technology, which in turn change according to new possibilities offered by knowledge.' At issue are not only the biases of ideology, but also the fact that the symbiosis between knowledge and ideology is affected by the very contingency of knowledge formation itself. We don't know what further knowledge new knowledge will beget. Thus, the authors claim that: 'One role that art can play is to suggest scenarios of "worlds under construction" and subvert technologies for the purpose of creating contestable futures, and exploring the variations that might have an effect' (ibid.).

It is Catts' view that 'our cultural evolution is much slower than our technological evolution' and, therefore, it is 'up to people – I suppose you could call them culture workers if you are dealing with culture – to try to bridge the gap between the culture and the technology in order for us as humans to deal with and be able to complain about what we are doing to ourselves, to the world and others' (2002). Bridging this gap is not about creating new certainties or assured knowledge. Catts also explains that the project has not only encountered unanticipated benefits, challenges, risks and ethical dilemmas, it has actively looked for them. For instance, the TC&A project prompted those involved to consider the 'aesthetics of care' and the obligations and responsibilities of generating, maintaining, exploiting and destroying semi-living beings. This is the uncomfortable terrain TC&A negotiates and 'One of the declared aims of SymbioticA is to convey the uneasiness we feel when we are dealing with living material cultures and why we think we're uncomfortable' (ibid.). Clearly, this discomfort is heightened by the fact that these artists do not only offer commentary on society and culture, but are engaged in the very processes they critique. In fact, they are engaged in a deconstructive process which exposes the aporia and paradox created by the economism, monetarism and performative adaptation in the knowledge economy and therefore the spectre of risk that haunts it. In this respect, the TC&A installations invoke the experience and undecidability of the ethico-political decision.

* * *

'The future can only be for ghosts' says Derrida (1994: 37). The risk economy problematizes innovation policy by revealing the uncertain future of social, political and cultural hazards ignored in the interest of commercial gain. The risk economy haunts the techno-economic logic of innovation policy. We have argued that the notion of risk is contextual and complex and that, as a consequence, understandings of the risk economy must encompass such complexity. The risk economy, in our view, involves an assemblage of 'certainties' and uncertainties, benefits and hazards. We have shown that different inflections of risk are produced by and distributed across the knowledge economy's central systems and subjects.

Techno-science and innovation systems are allegedly steered in the name of calculable risk, a notion that denies hazard and undecidability. But, we have demonstrated that these systems do in fact invoke risk as hazard in four main ways that go beyond the dangers produced by science itself. These are produced, first, through their unsafe compression of the relationship between time and scientific knowledge production; second, through their naïve notions of linear progress; third, through their blind acceptance of technological determinist thinking; and, fourth, through their obstinate refusal to see the contradictions between private profit and public interest.

The knowledge economy's central human subject, the technopreneur, also invokes multiple risk configurations. The technopreneur embodies the notion of risk as uncertainty. To the extent that s/he is involved in financial speculation s/he provokes risks that might be good or bad in money terms. However, given that the technopreneur is the personification of the knowledge economy itself, s/he also embodies the notion of risk as danger. Techno-artists are the leaky subjects of the knowledge economy; they slip out of its grasp and problematize its ideologies as our examples of the tissue culture projects illustrate. They too speak to the issue of risk as uncertainty but, unlike their technopreneurial colleagues, they deploy uncertainty to provoke ethical reflection.

Generally then, the ghost of the risk economy raises the possibility that the formula for economic growth in the knowledge economy may also endanger future generations. Risk as a calculus of probability and pretence to know the future actually conceals uncertainty. According to Reddy (1996: 222), 'the efficacy of social decision-making procedures to confront indeterminancy requires that "uncertainty" should take the place of "risk" as the governing motif of risk analysis'. To acknowledge uncertainty is to acknowledge that the future is unforeseeable and undecidable. And, to do this potentially opens the door to ethico-political decisions and responsibility for the future. For, according to Derrida (1994: 74–5), 'at a certain point promise and decision, which is to say responsibility, owe their possibility to the ordeal of undecidability which will always remain their condition'. The knowledge economy must live with this 'ordeal of undecidability'.

Notes

1 An ironical implication of such illusions of control and fantasies of progress is 'that unanticipated outcomes may be [seen as] the consequence of human action' (Lupton 1999: 6).
2 At the same time as Beck argues we have exceeded the capacity of the calculus of risk, the risk society thesis reiterates the 'rationalistic and instrumental-calculative model of risk' (Elliot 2002: 300) that he rejects. Based on cases of the manufactured hazards of modernization – pollution, disease, nuclear accidents and so forth – he enumerates, Beck's vision of the future is itself probabilistic even if the consequences of future hazards are incalculable.
3 By his own admission, Beck's (1999: 109) usage of the term reflexivity 'invites misunderstandings'. He suggests that it is in part a consequence of commonsense understandings of the term as denoting reflection and its usage by Giddens (1994) and Lash (1994) where it supposes knowledge or awareness of the problems of modernization. Thus, the type of self-confrontation reflexive modernization supposes 'should be clearly distinguished from the increase of knowledge and scientization in the sense of self-reflection on modernization' (Beck 1994: 6).
4 For a discussion of the implications of this policy for secondary school students in Australia, see Robb *et al.* (2003).
5 The dolls no longer exist as semi-living entities, but as images, and an invitation to visitors to post their worries (given that worry dolls are meant to solve worries) is on the Tissue Culture & Art website (www.tca.uwa.edu.au/guestbook/guest.asp).

3 The gift economy

> "But you were always a good man of business, Jacob," faultered [*sic*] Scrooge, who now began to apply this to himself.
> "Business!" cried the Ghost, wringing its hands again. "Mankind was my business. The common welfare was my business; charity, mercy, forbearance, and benevolence, were, all, my business. The dealings of my trade were but a drop of water in the comprehensive ocean of my business!"
>
> (Dickens, *A Christmas Carol*, [1843] 2003: 49)

Marley's ghost challenges Scrooge's idea of what counts as business, and suggests that it is more than an economic activity. It involves social as well as economic values, the 'common welfare' and the welfare of others. For Scrooge, the ghost's appearance initiates a radical reassessment of the business of business. What returns to Scrooge is a sense of community, a set of values and feelings that derive from social bonds, which are neither dependent on financial transactions, nor economic concerns. These beliefs, disavowed for the sake of money, reveal themselves to be far more valuable than any coming from the capitalist market, from commodity exchange.

The capitalist market is driven by the desire for wealth and the desire for material possessions or commodities. Marx critiques the capitalist mode of production, arguing it results in a loss of humanity and a sense of alienation as all social relationships are commodified. In the same way that another system of value haunts Scrooge, there is always, in any theory of materialism, a non-material presence. Hovering around money, around the material thing, is a value that is not material: 'Marx always described money, and more precisely the monetary sign, in the figure of appearance or simulacrum, more exactly of the ghost' (Derrida 1994: 45). This value and its problematic relation to material production haunts Marx; 'he thinks of nothing else' (ibid.: 10).

Drawing on Derrida, Jameson (1995: 102) explains:

> This is then Marx's fundamental mistake (if not 'error'): he wants to get rid of ghosts, he not only thinks he can do so, but that it is desirable to do

> so. But a world cleansed of spectrality is precisely ontology itself, a world of pure presence, of immediate density, of things without a past: for Derrida, an impossible and noxious nostalgia.

According to Jameson, there is an unacknowledged dependency on the spectre for Marx, a dependency that organizes the theory of materialism – a theory of value. At the heart of his theory of material reality is the disavowed haunting presence of the spectre. This is the presence that Marx attempts to '*conjure* (away)' (Derrida 1994: 47, original emphasis). This presence is invoked so that it can be expelled. Exorcism 'consists of repeating in the mode of an incantation that the dead man is really dead' (ibid.: 48). It is to ground the spectre in material reality, to take it back to the corpse, its origin. In exorcizing ghosts, in defending against them, the material, lifeless corpse of the past will be invoked.

In *Specters of Marx* (1994) Derrida examines contemporary attitudes towards Marxism (as we have indicated in our Foreshadowing). He speaks of the present as a time of a dominant discourse, the hegemony of an undifferentiated and omnipresent capitalism that incants the death of Marx, of Marxist ideology, of the Marxist state. He says, there is a 'manic, jubilatory' incantation that says: 'long live capitalism, long live the market, here's to the survival of economic and political liberalism' (ibid.: 52). However, although these incantations uphold the conquests of capitalism and declare that Marx(ism) is dead and buried, Derrida reminds us that the dead can return, they can come back to haunt us as ghosts.

The 'secure' foundations of the knowledge economy rest on the idea that commodity exchange, and its associated idea of self-interest, suffice as an explanation and as a motivation for the exchange and circulation of knowledge. What disturbs this notion is the presence of an archaic system of exchange, a gift economy. According to Callari, 'the gift … wears well a ghostly garb, haunting economics' (2002: 249). The gift economy recognizes spectres of the past: a system of exchange based upon the accumulation of social capital instead of financial capital; the person who gives, receives and repays for reasons of social obligation and community solidarity; the person who gains status and power through the act of giving; a community whose aim is to acquire relationships rather than money; a community whose values are social rather than individual.

In this chapter we examine several systems of gift exchange framed by a number of different theories of the gift that are primarily informed by Marcel Mauss' theory of the gift economy (first published 1925). In his interpretation of Mauss, Osteen suggests 'one of the primary challenges for gift theory has been to distinguish between gift exchanges and market exchanges, and thereby discriminate between gifts and commodities' (Osteen 2002a: 229). According to Mauss, members of a gift community are bound together in the obligatory circulation of meaningful objects. They are obligated in three ways: to give, to receive and to repay. This chapter argues that socially and ethically obligated exchange needs to be seen not as a contingent addendum to knowledge economy policy but as the positive manifestation of an inevitable other of commodity exchange.

Knowledge as a commodity

> What we're looking for is what's called monopoly rent, meaning it could either be protectable or not protectable ... There's a slight conflict ... with the academic ideal ... it also creates some tension between us and academics ... I'm trying to manage the expectations of both academics as well as the commercialization side.
>
> (Staff member, Research and Innovation section, Australian university)

In the knowledge economy we see the privileging of knowledge that can be commodified, codified, quantified and applied. In this context, knowledge is invariably understood in terms of economics. We therefore need to explain the economics of knowledge to fully understand the way knowledge operates in the knowledge economy. Knowledge is made valuable in the knowledge economy when it is reconceptualized as a commodity or good. However, knowledge functions differently from other commodities because it is symbolically constructed, not physically manufactured (although we acknowledge there are physical carriers of knowledge, such as paper, CDs, etc.). To clarify the properties of knowledge as a good, we will first outline the key properties of goods defined conventionally, using economic distinctions between 'rival' and 'non-rival', 'excludable' and 'non-excludable', and 'private' and 'public' goods.

Romer, a key New Growth economic theorist who we introduced in Chapter 1, defines a purely rival good as having the property 'that its use by one ... person precludes [or stops] its use by another' (1990: 73–4). In terms of physically manufactured goods, if two people share the object, then each person's potential use of it is reduced. Rival goods are a precondition for the economic notion of 'scarcity' as their depletion through consumption becomes the basis of a system of supply and demand that regulates a capitalist economy. As a symbolically constructed good, existing independently from physical objects, any number of people can use knowledge at the same time without it being depleted, and with no loss of benefits. In other words, one person's consumption of knowledge does not reduce the amount of knowledge available for others. Indeed it could be suggested that knowledge is essentially an inexhaustible resource that is actually enhanced through use or consumption. Jessop reiterates this point when he suggests 'the use-value of knowledge [as a] non-rival good does not diminish when that knowledge is shared' (2000: online). In economic terms, knowledge is a non-rival good as 'its use by one ... person in no way limits its use by another' (Romer 1990: 74).

If knowledge is a collectively shared, and collectively produced, non-depletable (or non-rival) good and the knowledge economy seeks to profit from and trade in knowledge, then knowledge 'first has to be made artificially scarce by being turned into a privately-owned commodity' (Kundnani 1998–9: 52). Thus, knowledge as an 'excludable' good becomes a key issue. Private commodities or goods are usually defined in terms of two characteristics: 'rival' (defined above) and 'excludable'. Romer states 'a good is excludable if the owner can prevent others from using it' (1990: 74). One of the key ways in which the owner of a good maintains a monopoly on that good, and controls access to it, is by charging people 'rent' for its use. One of the key determining factors of a private good is whether its supply can be profited from, whether non-payers can be excluded in a way that is profitable. Private goods are goods that are commercially exploitable (through trade and profit) in a capitalist market.

Public goods by contrast are non-rival (defined above) and non-excludable. A good is non-excludable if it is impossible to selectively exclude others from using it, if it is difficult to have monopoly ownership of that good and therefore make people pay for its use. Public goods are goods that are freely available to everybody. When a good is non-excludable its provision needs to be supplied by means other than the capitalist market if that good is deemed to be necessary or desirable. The level of supply of public goods is dependent on state intervention, and on the way in which the benefits of that good are valued within a community or nation (Kaul *et al.* 1999). This involves competing ideas of value within the political arena. Increased investment in certain public goods (for example, public libraries, galleries, museums) will only occur where there is consensus in powerful government circles about the value of public knowledge to society as a whole. It follows that the withdrawal of state support with respect to certain public goods will in part indicate a diminishment in political circles about the cultural or social value of that good. Of course, powerful lobby groups will influence policy agendas. Knowledge is a mixed good because it contains both public and private aspects. The idea that knowledge functions as both a public good and a private good will be demonstrated further by placing knowledge in a policy context.

A European Commission (2002c) statement addresses global public goods specifically, but their classifications apply to public goods in general. It identifies six main types, including knowledge. (The other five types are: environment, health, peace, security and governance.) It notes that global public goods 'bring advantages to society as a whole', whilst also suggesting that 'every individual has an equal entitlement' (ibid.: 1) to these goods. The notion of equity or 'fairness' reinforces the idea that as a public good, knowledge is a non-excludable entity. Knowledge 'has the potential to be enjoyed by all, regardless of whether the end user has paid for [it] or not' (ibid.). Kaul *et al.* (1999: 2) suggest that for knowledge to be a global public good it must satisfy these criteria:

- '[its] benefits have strong qualities of publicness – that is, [it is] marked by nonrivalry in consumption and nonexcludability';
- it must be relevant to more than one geographic region;
- its benefits must be enjoyed by a broad spectrum of classes;
- its use must not compromise future use.

A minimum definition of a global public good may be that it can benefit more than one group of countries, and that its benefits do not discriminate against particular groups of people, or future generations of people (Kaul *et al.* 1999).

Although, as its statement suggests, the European Commission has noble intentions in regard to knowledge as a public, non-excludable good, it also has commercial interests and therefore promotes knowledge as a private, excludable good. Jessop encapsulates the European Commission's approach to knowledge when he suggests there are 'contradiction[s] between knowledge as intellectual commons and [knowledge] as intellectual property' (2000: online). Drahos defines the intellectual commons as 'an independently existing resource which is open to use' (1996: 54).

At the 2005 European Council, European heads of state and government affirmed their commitment to 'increasing the potential for economic growth and of strengthening European competitiveness by investing above all in knowledge, innovation and human capital' (European Commission 2005a: 3). In this statement, knowledge is also linked to 'social cohesion', 'social sustainability', and the chance for Europe to 'strengthen its model of society' (ibid.: 2). However, the declared way to achieve these aims is by fundamentally economic means. This investment in knowledge is recognized as being crucial in making 'Europe the most dynamic and competitive, knowledge-based economy in the world' (ibid.: 2).[1] Some of the key ways in which the European Commission intends to achieve these aims is by: expanding research and development 'to 3% of EU GDP, two thirds of which should come from private investment[;] introducing fiscal incentives for research, and innovation[;] . . . improving and adapting intellectual property rights [IPR] regimes[; and] strengthening links between universities and industry' (ibid.: 3). The clear implication is that investing in knowledge means raising the capacity to both produce and exploit knowledge in a market situation. For example, intellectual property rights protect 'the investment which firms make in research and development by guaranteeing them a monopoly on the exploitation of knowledge arising out of their research' (Kundnani 1998–99: 52). Therefore the European Commission's push towards commodified knowledge will ultimately 'help overcome Europe's weakness in commercialising the results of research' (European Commission 2005a: 8).

As the European Commission is striving to make knowledge profitable (its consumption and circulation dependent on payment) it thereby excludes non-payers. When knowledge is marketed and monopolized it becomes a private good. It is no longer a public good available to all, but rather a tradable commodity available only to those who pay for its use. In broader terms, given that making money from knowledge is the essence of the knowledge economy, it follows that the knowledge economy will inevitably involve the privatization of the intellectual commons and the potential exclusion of non-payers from the common pool of knowledge.

Knowledge is vulnerable to contestations over its meaning and value. Powerful interests compete over the merits of such things as the extent to which knowledge should be considered a public or private good. Compromises between such sets of interests may in effect mean that knowledge takes the form of a mixed good, being both public and private, or that policy bodies adopt profoundly contradictory policies, as in the case of the European Commission. In the present era of the knowledge economy, one of the sites of this struggle over the meaning and value of knowledge is in the area of intellectual property rights. Whilst knowledge may be a public good, and non-rival in its conceptual form, it can be excluded from other public users via IPR (as the European Commission statement demonstrates).

Intellectual property rights and the knowledge economy

> What needs to happen is that more and more researchers understand what IP [intellectual property] is and what might be generated during the course of their research ... The other pressure is coming from the agencies themselves including the ARC [Australian Research Council] ... they are very keen to see that we are effectively identifying IP that might be of value and managing it so that they are in a better position to show the impact that their research is actually having.
>
> (Staff member, Research and Innovation section, Australian university)

In the knowledge economy, knowledge can produce financial and other benefits. Individuals identify their ownership of knowledge using *intellectual property*. *Intellectual property rights* is 'the term used to refer to the system of law in place designed to allow people to protect and exploit their IP'. There are four categories of IPR: 'patents (for inventions); trademarks (for brand identity); designs (for product appearance); and copyright (for material such as literary and artistic outputs, music, films, sound recordings, broadcasts, software and multimedia)' (Epstein, Kenway and Boden 2005: 49; for problems of copyright see Carrick 2004). IPR mean that the owner of knowledge can claim it, and then charge for it. As a result, strict boundaries are applied to the dissemination of knowledge. The owner of knowledge can prevent others from using their idea, and thus knowledge becomes excludable, a private good available only to those who are prepared to pay for it.[2]

Intellectual property rights are central to the innovation agenda (see Chapter 2), which is pivotal in knowledge economy policies. OECD policy, for example, endorses a strong IPR régime. This discussion paper typifies its position and the widespread claims made about IPR:

> Intellectual property helped make possible the conditions for innovation, entrepreneurship and market-oriented economic growth that shaped the 20th Century. In the 21st Century, IPRs increasingly will define these conditions, and will dictate the pace and direction of innovation, investment and economic growth around the world.
>
> (OECD 2003: 6)

According to the OECD paper, IPR provide 'a powerful *incentive* for creating things' (ibid.: 13, emphasis added). In other words, it is the possibility to profit from new ideas that encourages knowledge production in the first place. The position of IPR in innovation policy is also summarized in the UK government's 'Innovation Report', which states that IPR

> underpin innovation by providing a tool for business to make a return on its investment. For many innovators, access to finance is impossible without IP protection ... IP laws aim to strike the right balance between protecting new developments and stimulating competition.
>
> (Department of Trade and Industry (UK) 2003: 73)

This is an often-repeated claim made on behalf of IPR, but it is not uncontested. Arguments can be mounted that the history of knowledge production (such as basic research and creative endeavour which generates new ideas) suggests that it is not motivated by the financial protection offered by IPR. It could also be argued that universities, rather than IPR régimes, have been the key to an innovation process that requires knowledge. Furthermore, even where IPR play a role in innovation, this role is overshadowed by the fact that these companies initially rely on public knowledge produced by universities (Drahos and Braithwaite 2002).

However, knowledge production in universities is also increasingly coming under the control and influence of IPR, particularly through the commercialization agenda promoted by innovation policy (see Chapter 2). When government funding of knowledge production in universities is tied to the gaining of IPR, universities are put under enormous pressure to participate in the privatization of the intellectual commons and the free movement of knowledge (ibid.). Such pressure takes various forms and has various possible adverse consequences which Drahos and Braithwaite discuss at length. Some potential dangers in terms of innovation policy relate to research links with industry. For example, delivering adverse findings to an industry partner may lead the partner to attempt to discredit or hide the findings (see, for example, Krimsky 2003). Further, when a university 'cedes its research priorities to corporate sponsors it is not likely to pursue questions that have no patentable outcome' (Bollier 2002: 144). Clearly, when only 'profitable' research is pursued, certain knowledges may be neglected and the circulation of knowledge is restricted.

Although shortcomings in measuring innovation through the production of IPR are acknowledged in some policy circles and are being addressed (OECD 2003), the overall trajectory is still the same. In terms of universities, knowledge production that can be measured in economic terms is part of the innovation process, knowledge production that cannot is outside the loop, and this typically refers to knowledge production within the arts, social science and humanities disciplines. As we argue in Chapter 4, it is not necessarily always in the interests of the arts to frame themselves within the commercialization agenda. However, within the arts disciplines there is a visible shift towards knowledge production that conforms to the commercialization agenda promoted by innovation policy (see Chapter 4; see also Bullen *et al.* 2004a, Kenway *et al.* 2004b).

Of course it is not only the integrity of academic research that is at stake because of IPR, but also the survival of the academic intellectual community. In terms of knowledge networks, when knowledge is a tradable asset, so too are its associated relationships. These are conceived instrumentally and commercially; in other words, in terms of use and exchange value. Other people or groups are evaluated in terms of what they can trade. They may be valued because they can back-fill the knowledge or the status that a particular knowledge network lacks and needs in order to competitively bid for resources. It is perhaps a misinterpretation in policy of the nature of an academic community that is at the heart of the problem. What is being suppressed in this misunderstanding is an acknowledgement that an academic community and other knowledge communities also have the potential to function as gift economies, although they do not always function in this manner. It is this possibility that the haunting of the knowledge economy brings to light.

Knowledge communities and gift economies

> The limitations of intellectual property [are] that knowledge ... can't really be treated as property ... and that a great deal of the exchange of knowledge is actually not traded activity.
>
> (Staff member, Strategy and Analysis, National Office of the Information Economy [Australian Commonwealth Government])

In the following discussion we consider Mauss' theorization of the gift and apply it to the contemporary academic community in the context of knowledge economy policy.[3] Literature on the gift is extensive and it is not our intention to summarize it all here.[4] Our method rather is to sketch some of the key elements of gift theory as outlined in Mauss' seminal work *The Gift: the form and reason for exchange in archaic societies* (first published

1925) which focuses on systems of exchange within so-called 'primitive' societies.

According to Mauss, members of a gift community are bound together in the obligatory circulation of meaningful objects. They are obligated in three ways: to give, to receive and to repay for reasons of community, solidarity and status. The obligation towards another, the obligation to return without diminishing social relationships, is the key to understanding the gift. It is this force that makes the gift 'one of the bases of social life' (Mauss [1925] 1990: 4). Gift exchange binds objects and subjects in a symbolic and reciprocal relationship that delimits their movements according to social and ethical codes.

Mauss develops his theory of the gift economy around a principle of reciprocity. He asks: 'What power resides in the object given that causes its recipient to pay it back?' (ibid.: 3). He derives his understanding of this force from the Maori concept of *hau*, the spirit of a specific person that is transferred in part to the objects they give. Mauss (ibid.: 33) states:

> [O]bligation ... takes the form of interest in the objects exchanged; the objects are never completely separated from the men who exchange them; the communion and alliance they establish are well-nigh indissoluble.

The *hau* is the spiritual power of given objects. According to Mauss it is 'the spirit of the gift' (ibid.: 10). The term 'spirit' is found throughout Mauss' work on the gift. Osteen defines 'spirit' as 'an immaterial aura of connection to other humans and to something greater than any human individual' (2002a: 244). As part of the giver's spirit is embodied in the given object, it is driven to return to its place of origin, to come back to the person giving. The *hau* of an object cannot be accumulated by someone to whom it does not belong. It is not something that can be alienated from its place within a particular social network. Mauss ([1925] 1990: 12) explains:

> to give something is to give part of oneself ... [one gives] away what is in reality part of one's nature and substance, while to receive something is to receive part of someone else's spiritual essence.

In gift exchange, the *hau* can leave a person through the medium of the gift, but can only do so in a temporary way through a process of circulating within a group, and it must then return to its point of origin. This return can only be realized 'through the medium of an object given in exchange for the original gift' (Yan 2002: 67). In this way the continuous exchange of gifts serves to fulfil the obligation to give, to receive and to repay in a gift economy.

At the heart of any gift giving is the 'good gift':

> A good gift is something like an act of recognition, in which the donor makes her knowledge of the recipient known to the recipient, who in

> turn may come to recognise something new about herself, or the donor, or the relationship. The desire to surprise and be surprised arises out of this deeper desire to know and be known by another.
>
> (Fennell 2002: 94)

The 'good gift' partakes in an intimate knowledge of and between people. When a gift is presented to another, and when that gift has attached to it some form of knowledge about the other, what is being affirmed is a form of social or communal knowledge. Objects cannot be 'given as gifts outside of the group without threatening the very social identities that underpin their inalienability' (Osteen 2002b: 235). The act of giving away an object associated with a specific person or group demonstrates a fundamental paradox in a gift economy. Gift giving involves a separation from and belonging to its origin point. Objects that are exchanged in a gift economy are imbued with the spirit of the person giving, the people who are linked into the circulation and history of that object, and the community and related communities. We might argue that this process reverses Marx's theory of commodity fetishism. In a commodity economy, the people who produce the things are transformed and appear to be objective characteristics of the things themselves (Marx 1915). In a gift economy, the things that people give contain the subjective characteristics of the people giving and the social identity of their community. As Osteen suggests, 'in a gift economy, objects are personified; in a market economy, persons are objectified' (Osteen 2002b: 233).

Marx asserts that commodity exchange moved from the margins to the 'interior of the community, exerting a disintegrating influence upon it' ([1859] 1971: 50). We could also say that commodity exchange exerts a disintegrating influence on the *spirit* and the social bonds of a community. When objects are sold in a commodity economy the ownership rights of the object are transferred to the new owner. Therefore the object is fully dissociated or 'alienated' from the original owner. In contrast, 'gifts are concrete representations of social relations' (Osteen 2002b: 2). As 'inalienable' objects, gifts serve to nurture the *spirit* and cement the social bonds of community. Gregory (1982: 19)[5] maintains the aim of gift giving is to acquire relationships rather than money, social capital not economic capital:

> The gift economy, then, is a debt economy. The aim of a transactor in such an economy is to acquire as many gift-debtors as she possibly can and not to maximise profit, as it is in the commodity economy. What a gift transactor desires is the personal relationships that the exchange of gifts creates, and not the things themselves.

Within capitalism people are required to accumulate economic power by amassing incomings; the gift giver aims to amass social credit amongst their group through expenditure. In this sense, we discover a theory of gift exchange by inverting the fundamentals of commodity exchange. Where there is gift exchange, at least according to Gregory, there can be no commodity exchange.[6]

There are two major knowledge requirements necessary in a gift economy: knowledge of the social system of obligation, and knowledge of the spiritual essence of the gift. We may also say that this knowledge does not consider society and the spiritual from a distance. These things are not objects for a disinterested person's consideration. Neither does knowledge belong only to the individual. It belongs to the social and spiritual realm, to which it must always return. These are the constitutive elements of knowledge in a gift economy. Social knowledge starts with the idea that all members of that society are socially obligated, or potentially socially obligated, that they are all in relations, or contracts with each other of debt and credit. Spiritual knowledge pertains to the idea that the object is imbued with a particular essence when it is exchanged that is derived from the gift-giver and their community. As this spirit cannot be alienated from the original gift-giver and their community, the gift itself is compelled to return to its place of origin. In a gift economy, knowledge is forever tied to the individual and the community; so too is its expression, or the material products of its expression. Here we find a key distinction between knowledge within a gift economy and knowledge within a commodity economy. As Gregory maintains, 'commodities are *alienable* objects transacted by aliens; gifts are *inalienable* objects transacted by non-aliens' (ibid.: 43, original emphases).

Knowledge communities as gift communities

> Just to what extent should knowledge be a shared resource or common resource, and to what extent is it actually property? I see that debate at the moment as being one of the things that will ... actually help clarify the term [knowledge economy] ... There's a big difference between a private benefit to a patent holder and the public interest in the wider diffusion of knowledge across the economy and society.
>
> (Staff member, Strategy and Analysis, National Office of the Information Economy [Australian Commonwealth Government])

Knowledge communities do not only consist of formal academic and research communities. They also include informal knowledge networks of lay people. DIPEx, for example, is a not-for-profit open access health information website where people talk about their experiences of illness. Patients, their carers, family and friends, doctors, nurses and other health professionals contribute to it and then benefit from the personal knowledge that is offered by others with the same illnesses. The DIPEx home-page (2005: online) states:

> Being told you have an illness can be confusing and frightening and finding reliable information can be frustrating. DIPEx shows you a variety of personal experiences of health and illness. You can watch, listen to or read their interviews, find reliable information on treatment choices and where to find support.

We suggest that this form of knowledge sharing results in the creation of a knowledge community and illustrates one model of a gift community. The DIPEx forum is the place where people can discuss their experiences of health and illness, ask questions, and pass on advice to others. Here knowledge is the meaningful object that circulates freely within a group of people. The forum states, 'the DIPEx community is your space, where you can have your say' (ibid.). As a result of giving the gift of knowledge, the social bonds of that community are strengthened. It is this equitable interface between users and producers of knowledge which de-traditionalizes knowledge hierarchies. As knowledge about the experiences of illness is exchanged from one patient to another, medical experts are no longer the sole source of information, rather, the patients themselves also become a source of expertise. They become 'lay experts'.

According to one of its staff members, the Centre for Educational Research and Innovation (OECD) is 'very interested in what we call knowledge communities'. He says 'medical lay experts' collect valuable data and they 'are really part of the scientific process of knowledge production and research'. He cites initiatives similar to DIPEx whereby the free exchange of knowledge between patients and others means that knowledge is given as a gift. However, this does not mean that all such knowledge networks are free of self-interest or a commercial agenda. In the example of a knowledge community given by the interviewee, parents of children with genetic and other conditions collect the research data. This data facilitates scientific research and one possible outcome is that this initial knowledge may expedite the discovery of a patented treatment. Whether benefits are shared equally between lay people and experts remains a question that is not addressed. Commercialization means a shift from gift to market exchange. Presumably, if the original knowledge contributors want to treat their illness, they will then have to buy this knowledge back in the form of a pharmaceutical cure.

A staff member of the Trade Union Advisory Committee discusses the patenting of medical knowledge in regard to the General Agreement of Trade in Services (GATS) and the domain of health. He states 'everyday life in the end will be affected by ... powerful moves towards privatization in the provision of services'. Thus, as the OECD staff member maintains, although the 'cost of collating the data on the disease [by scientists] is really low, [and] it is efficient to involve [lay people] in this process', the possible economic gains to be made from this knowledge are potentially high. It is these knowledge profits that the knowledge economy as a commodity economy exploits. To paraphrase Gregory, where there is commodity exchange there can be no gift exchange. As the unequal exchange of knowledge in the knowledge economy triumphs over the equitable exchange of knowledge in the gift economy, respective distinctions are made between knowledge users and knowledge producers, on the basis of those who pay for these services and those who profit from them. This is also the case with the knowledge community of the university.

According to Stiglitz, 'initial knowledge is a key input into the production of further knowledge' (1999: 312). In other words, new knowledge arises from working on and with the ideas of others. In terms of an intellectual community such as the university, the academic receives knowledge from others, adds their own intellectual contribution, and then returns this transformed knowledge to this community. One way this happens is through the publication of research literature. As we stated earlier, the use of knowledge as a non-rival good does not reduce the amount of knowledge available for others. We suggested that knowledge is essentially an inexhaustible resource that is actually enhanced through consumption. The publication of research literature facilitates the circulation of knowledge, and the continuance of an intellectual community. In this respect, there are parallels to be made between the way the circulation of knowledge sustains an intellectual community, and the way the circulation of gifts maintains a gift community. Research literature disseminates ideas that have been reworked, or refined and given back to the intellectual community. Research functions by receiving the gift of knowledge from others, and then giving the gift of knowledge back in return in the form of publications.

A scholarly community has well-developed protocols for fulfilling the three obligations of the gift by: giving (contributing new knowledge through research publications); receiving (using initial knowledge to produce new knowledge); and repaying debt (citation). Citation rules and practices are community building because individuals acknowledge others within that community. Citation rules and practices establish, continue and develop relationships within a body of knowledge and define that disciplinary community to itself and to the outside. As such, they can be thought of as one aspect of a gift economy characterized as a 'debt economy'. Indeed, the language associated with citations, or more particularly with student handbooks explaining the practice of citation, most commonly uses economic metaphors to illuminate the process. Citations are a sign that we *acknowledge a debt* to another, that we *give credit*, and to not cite (to plagarize) is to *steal*. It also involves, importantly, the idea that the thing given is not alienated from the person or the group. By participating in the three obligations of the gift, the academic contributes to the maintenance of the terms of exchange of knowledge. Indeed, a gift community is in large part defined by the presence of obligated social relationships. Anyone who fails to enact the three obligations is 'effectively denying that he or she is in a social relationship' (Carrier 1995: 21), and is consequently affirming the end of that relationship. While it may well be the case that not all scholarly communities operate in this manner – for example, contemporary performative and audit cultures in the academy individualize effort and undermine trust (Strathern 2000) – it can nonetheless be argued that the gift ideal is what holds the real together. The three obligations are the ways that the community reaffirms itself to itself.

If an intellectual community is dependent on a gift economy, then it follows that knowledge economy policy needs to theorize itself in terms of the gift as well as the commodity. This means that it needs to advocate on behalf of the one who gives, receives and repays knowledge for reasons of obligation to knowledge itself, and solidarity towards an on-going intellectual community. As Frow (1997: 104) explains:

> Gift exchange is at the core of social cohesion, or rather it represents a social generosity that is absent from other, more 'contractual' or 'mechanical' forms of social solidarity. One of the main functions of the theory of the gift has accordingly been to provide an account of altruism or of non-exploitative reciprocity as the basis of community.

The idea that the gift is the property of no one and the property of all implies that knowledge as a gift belongs to the intellectual commons. Any system that is founded on this principle maintains the intellectual gift community. In the era of the knowledge economy we argue that asserting the legitimacy of such a system represents a haunting within the dominant paradigm of commercialism and economic self-interest. Support for such a system can be witnessed in a number of public knowledge schemes, such as the Public Knowledge Project at the University of British Columbia, the Open Source Initiative, and the endorsement of Open Access (OA), particularly in terms of research literature. These have arisen in response to a worrying trend in scholarly publishing, as we will now explain.

Scholarly publishing and open access

Scholarly publishing (particularly in peer-reviewed journals available online through institutional subscription) is perhaps the key contemporary avenue for the circulation of knowledge within academic communities. Of concern is scholarly publication where knowledge goods become excludable to various populations, not just to a general public, but also to sections of the scholarly community, including those in different geographical regions where costs might be prohibitive. While the legal basis of the exclusion is the assignment of copyright, this does not necessarily mean that access need be restricted. The main issue is that the assignment of copyright to publishers then allows journals to charge all users a fee to access the work; or in some cases, even to access the abstract. At the heart of the issue is the abuse of IPR and the commercialization of knowledge.

The big publishing houses are currently 'amassing huge electronic archives of intellectual property' and 'buying each other up, merging and accumulating all the world's books, archives, research, journals into an every-decreasing number of corporations' (Australian Broadcasting Corporation 2001b: online). Why? The answer is the potential for profit, and there is much profit to be made. For North American research libraries, journal costs rose by 227% between 1986 and 2002; while in the UK journal costs rose 159% between 1991–2001 (Association of Research Libraries 2003: online). Of course, the more journals the publishing house has, the more it is able to charge. And once it has a monopoly in a particular field, the opportunities for additional charges increase. There is potential for viewing, sharing and downloading opportunities to be further restricted and thus to be increasingly costly. In essence we are seeing the increasing commodification and privatization of public knowledge in the digitizing and globalizing intellectual bazaar.

While this process may enhance the distribution of knowledge, access may become more and more restricted as it becomes more and more costly. Thus, while the knowledge economy can capitalize on the non-rival status of knowledge, its push to exclude is self-defeating. Of equal concern is the fact that the control of knowledge slips yet further from the hands of those who produce it, and from those who fund those who produce it, namely tax-payers. Whilst publishing houses have increased their profits, university libraries have simultaneously cancelled journal purchases while accepting costly, and perhaps even unnecessary, 'Big Deal' journal bundles. This places pressure on Library funds to reduce expenditure elsewhere, most obviously in other areas of scholarly publishing (Johnson 2004).

Whilst academics write and peer-review the articles that go into the research journals (usually without payment), their university may then have to pay to view them. University libraries spend a large percentage of their acquisitions budget on electronic journal subscriptions. The irony here is that universities, and tax-payers, in the case of public universities, are paying for knowledge three times: to produce it, to review it and then to purchase it. Therefore publicly funded knowledge is turned into an excludable good. Those outside the university sector and indeed those in poor institutions and poor countries around the world find themselves excluded from ready access knowledge.

Academics, librarians, and extended coalitions, have recognized the threat that this commercial régime poses to them. Velterop (2005: 7), an academic who has developed a practical guide to OA for scholarly societies, states:

> The currently prevalent model of subscription-based journals is not achieving the goal of optimising the return on the research investment that the world makes. Limited access means limited use, limited impact, and limited benefits for ... society at large.

Perhaps the best example of the academic resistance to the commercialization of knowledge can be found in the support for OA research literature. This endorsement can be seen as an assertion of the research community as a gift community. OA literature is digital, online, free of charge, and free of most copyright and licensing restrictions.

The term 'open access' was first defined in the *Budapest Open Access Initiative* (Open Society Institute 2002; see also 'Berlin 3 Open Access: Progress in Implementing the Berlin Declaration on Open Access to Knowledge in the Sciences and Humanities' (2005)), the result of a meeting in Budapest of supporters of OA who were brought together by the Open Society Institute (OSI) in late 2001. Its members include academics and a broad range of representatives from libraries, publishing coalitions and scientific associations. The Initiative, which focuses primarily on peer-reviewed journal articles, characterizes OA research literature as that which makes

> free availability on the public internet [the norm], permitting any users to read, download, copy, distribute, print, search or link to the full texts of these articles, crawl [*sic*] them for indexing, pass them as data to software, or use them for any other lawful purpose, without financial, legal or technical barriers.
>
> (Open Society Institute 2002: online; for an expanded definition of OA see *Berlin Declaration* (Max Planck Society 2003: online))

The Bethesda Statement followed the Budapest Open Access Initiative in 2003. This statement was the result of a meeting of scientists, funding agencies, librarians, scientific societies and publishers convened by the Howard Hughes Medical Institute and the Wellcome Trust. In essence, the definition in the Bethesda Statement is the same as the one in the Budapest Initiative, with a focus more on actual legal and practical consequences. In 2003, the Max Planck Society in Germany also convened a meeting on 'Open Access to Knowledge in the Sciences and Humanities'. This meeting widened the discussion by including the humanities and produced the Berlin Declaration on OA. This again is substantially the same as the Bethesda Statement.

This endorsement of OA is the means through which an academic community can continue to flourish along the lines of a gift economy. By making knowledge freely available, and easily and equitably accessible to the public it fulfils the three obligations of the gift: to give, to receive and to repay. OA is a ground-swell movement emanating from the academic community in reaction to the negative impacts of the commercialization of knowledge. It removes price barriers (subscriptions, licensing fees, pay-per-view fees) and permission barriers (most copyright and licensing restrictions). OA does not close knowledge off from the intellectual commons by making knowledge an excludable commodity. Rather it 'closes [the] gaps in access to knowledge' (Velterop 2005: 7) by making it available for all. The only way to sustain the intellectual commons (for the present and the future) is to give back to it as much, if not more, than one has taken; and to not preclude others from similar use. OA to knowledge is a 'good gift' that sustains the academic community as it 'enables the building of databases and knowledge-bases' (ibid.).

The Public Knowledge Project is also concerned about the privatization of public knowledge. Its goal is to expand the public reach and value of academic research. The project seeks to understand the potential contribution new technologies will make to knowledge's public sphere. It 'is dedicated to exploring whether and how new technologies can be used to improve the professional and public value of scholarly research'. The project aims 'to improve both scholarly quality and public accessibility' through enhanced online infrastructure and knowledge management strategies. It has an overall commitment to 'the collaborative potential of knowledge sharing among communities of interest' (2005: online), including professionals, practitioners, researchers, policy-makers, and the public. Some of the project's initiatives include: 'Improving the Value of Research for Policy-makers, Journalists, and the Public' (2001–3); 'Extending the Global Knowledge Exchange: Technological Change and the Research Capacities of Developing Nations' (2003–4); and 'Supporting the Reading of Research in Online Settings' (2004–7).

Whilst the Public Knowledge Project focuses specifically on OA to scholarly research, the Open Source Initiative is a non-profit corporation dedicated to managing and promoting open source software for the good of the community as a whole. 'The basic idea behind open source is very simple: When programmers can read, redistribute, and modify the source code for a piece of software, the software evolves. People improve it, people adapt it, people fix bugs.' The open source community maintains that 'this rapid evolutionary process produces better software than the traditional closed model' (2005: online). Some examples of open source software include: operating systems such as Linux, FreeBSD, OpenBSD, and NetBSD; Internet applications such as Mozilla, Apache and BIND; and programming tools such as Perl, Zope, and PHP.

Into the realm of the governmental

We are currently seeing governmental bodies finally paying attention to activist projects, and the way in which they promote the free exchange of knowledge as a gift. But, as we will explain, although OA is now on the governmental agenda, there are still those who seek to question how truly open access to knowledge will become.

In 2004, the European Commission (2005b: online) launched a study on the economic and technical evolution of the scientific publication markets in Europe, the results of which were made available in 2006. The study identified measures at European level which could help to improve conditions governing access to and the exchange, dissemination and archiving of scientific publications while guaranteeing a high level of quality, diversity and protection of authors' rights. In 2004, the OECD also issued a *Declaration on Access to Research Data from Public Funding* (2004b: online) that focuses on the benefits of OA particularly in relation to scientific research and innovation. Furthermore, in the same year, the Group of Eight vice-chancellors, representing Australia's pre-eminent research universities, recorded 'their commitment to open access initiatives that will enhance access to scholarly information for the public good' (ibid.) in their universities.

Another recent development is the *Position Statement on Access to Research Outputs* issued by the Research Councils UK (RCUK) (2005: online). The eight UK Research Councils operate across all disciplines under the umbrella of RCUK. This position statement outlines the Research Councils' views on the dissemination of and access to research outputs (for full details of RCUK Position Statement on Access to Research Outputs see RCUK 2005: online). In summary, the RCUK is committed to:

- making ideas and knowledge derived from publicly-funded research freely available and accessible for public use;
- guaranteeing quality assurance by ensuring effective mechanisms such as peer-review are in place;
- providing efficient and cost-effective use of public funds for the models and mechanisms for publication and access to research results;
- ensuring that the output from current and future research are preserved and remain accessible for future generations.

(Ibid.)

The Research Councils are the first public funding agencies in the world to mandate OA with regard to the results of council-funded research, with access to this research literature facilitated by Internet technologies. The RCUK advocates communication, access and availability of research literature through e-print repositories and open access journals.

E-print repositories are either institutional or subject-based digital collections of research literature. (For the purposes of our argument we will restrict our focus to institutional repositories.) Institutional repositories preserve the intellectual output of a single university or a multiple institution community of colleges and universities. According to Crow (2002: 3), a Senior Consultant for the Scholarly Publishing and Academic Resources Coalition (SPARC), they

> provide a critical catalyst ... in reforming the system of scholarly communication by expanding access to research ... [and] have the potential to serve as tangible indicators of an institution's quality ... [and] the

> relevance of its research activities, thus increasing the institution's visibility, status and public value.

Institutional repositories can therefore be thought of as the building blocks of the academic community as a gift community. Ideally they will become part of 'a global system of distributed, interoperable repositories that provides the foundations for a new disaggregated model of scholarly publishing' (Crow 2002: 4). As they centralize, preserve and make freely accessible a university's intellectual capital, they do not diminish social relations, but rather consolidate them by affirming the scholarly community, academic solidarity and academic status.

The RCUK statement also maintains it will ensure that published research remains of a high quality by instituting rigorous peer-review, further recommending that e-print repositories make a clear distinction between published research that has and has not been peer-reviewed. In most research disciplines the editors and referees who perform peer-review donate their labour without expecting payment. In this respect, peer-review in an academic community (at both OA journals and conventional journals) is another form of gift giving, whereby altruism and non-exploitative reciprocity become the basis of a gift community.

The Research Councils further recommend the adoption of an 'author-pays' publication model. SPARC acknowledges that the term 'author-pays' is misleading. However, in the RCUK position statement, this remark is further qualified by stating: research 'grantees who choose to publish in OA journals that charge author-side processing fees may pay the fees out of their grants' (2005: online). (It is noted in the statement, however, that 'the viability of this funding model is sufficiently uncertain that the RCUK was not persuaded to set up a special fund ... to pay these fees' (ibid.).) Therefore, OA does not necessarily convert the user-pays system (endorsed by big publishing houses) to an author-pays system, rather the OA publication model is funded by the public to ensure knowledge remains a public good. The final point made by the RCUK is in the interests of long-term preservation, whereby the British Library and other Legal Deposit Libraries are acknowledged as having a critical role to play in the preservation of digital publications.

SPARC (2005: online) has responded to the RCUK position statement by saying:

> The policy is superb. It has four primary strengths. First, it mandates OA and does not merely request it. Second, it applies to all publicly-funded research, not just biomedicine. Third, it gives authors some flexibility about the OA archive in which to deposit their work. Fourth, it offers to pay fees at OA journals that charge fees.

Not surprisingly, the Association of Learned and Professional Society

Publishers (ALPSP) have responded more cautiously. Their chief concern is that the immediate publication of OA research literature in e-print repositories may economically weaken peer-reviewed journals. They state 'any new model which has the potential to "siphon off" a significant percentage of otherwise paying customers will, understandably, undermine the financial viability of [peer-reviewed journals'] value-adding activities' (2005: online). Some examples include: 'commissioning editorials, reviews and opinion pieces which put the original research articles in context ...; ensuring maximum visibility of the journals' content, through secondary databases, search engines and elsewhere; [and investing] in robust and sophisticated journal delivery platforms' (ibid.). They further suggest that 'alternative licensing and business models ... are necessary if the system is not to be gravely damaged' (ibid.). In this context, economic concerns are privileged over social relationships. By advocating that OA proves itself as 'a viable business model' (ibid.), a misunderstanding of the possible ways in which an academic community can function is again reinforced. It is this possibility that the haunting spectre of the gift reveals.

* * *

Haunting the knowledge economy is an 'archaic' gift economy that uses the technology of the present to question its future direction. The notion of Open Access, particularly the push towards OA research literature, demonstrates key features of a gift economy. In this system, if knowledge is used then its use must also be repaid, or returned to the site of circulation (i.e. go back into e-print repositories and open access journals). In a gift economy, there is an obligation to return to the community what one has taken, with interest. With OA the academic community is joined together in a non-commodified and obligated way. What belongs to this gift community is given, and yet stays within that community. The part of oneself that the academic gives away is their knowledge, that which substantiates their status in the academic community in the first place. In this context, the gift is the property of no one and the property of all. We have shown that knowledge as a gift belongs to the intellectual commons. Whilst knowledge in the knowledge economy is a commodity or private good determined by intellectual property.

The knowledge economy asserts a need to commodify knowledge and to protect knowledge profits through intellectual property rights. We have argued that these rights will essentially restrict access to knowledge to those who can afford to pay. These rights will harm academic standards, slow the circulation of research and diminish the pool of available knowledge. What they will do in effect is destroy the substance that they wish to exploit: knowledge. We have suggested that resistance is presently gathering against this process involving free and open access to research literature using the Internet. As the Budapest Open Access Initiative states, 'An old tradition and a new technology have converged to make possible an unprecedented public good' (Open Society Institute 2002: online).

We have raised the idea that the aim of the gift giver in an intellectual gift economy, such as the OA community, is to acquire as many intellectual-debtors as possible, not to maximize private profit, as it is in the commodity economy. In other words, the aim of gift giving is to acquire relationships rather than money, social capital not economic capital. To demonstrate this notion we have mobilized Gregory's suggestion that the gift economy is a debt economy (1982). What a gift transactor desires is an intellectual community, the intellectual relationships that the exchange of gifts creates and not the things themselves. The ideal subject of knowledge economy discourse – the technopreneur – finds such notions incomprehensible and even reprehensible. Debating if and how these two different subject positions might accommodate each other is vital to the future of knowledge production.

The ghost of the gift economy is an inheritance from the past. According to Derrida, 'there is no inheritance without a call to obligation and responsibility. An inheritance is always the affirmation of a debt.' It affirms the notion that 'we must always return more than we receive' (1994: 91–2). Derrida argues further that:

> Inheritance is never a *given*, it is always a task ... All questions on the subject of being or of what is to be (or not to be) are questions of inheritance ... That we *are* heirs does not mean that we *have* or that we *receive* this or that, some inheritance that enriches us one day with this or that, but that the *being* of what we are *is* first of all inheritance, whether we like it or know it or not.
>
> (Ibid., original emphases)

The inheritance of the gift economy haunts the knowledge economy whether it likes it or knows it or not.

Notes

1 The central action to support the development of the European knowledge economy is the Seventh Research Framework Programme emphasizing investment in research – 'the driver for the production and exploitation of knowledge' (European Commission 2005a: 2) and development. For details on the European Commission's Sixth Framework Programme, particularly its funding of Networks of Excellence, see Kenway *et al.* 2004a.

2 IPR are protected by the state. In other words, the state must police the legal and illegal use of commercialized knowledge. As we will demonstrate later (in Chapter 5), under the recent TRIPS (Trade-Related Intellectual Property Rights) agreement this applies on a global scale to all World Trade Organization (WTO) members.

3 One of the persistent concerns in theories of the gift, and one that we will not pursue here, is that of the 'potlatch' or 'waste'. Our concern here is with co-operative rather than competitive gift exchange. Our focus is on those activities in a gift economy that are primarily motivated by the desire of its members to enhance that community. Rivalrous gift exchange, as expounded by Mauss ([1925] 1990) in his discussion of the 'potlatch' and by Bataille (1988–91) in terms of destruction,

sacrifice and waste have more to do with claims for individual power and prestige within the community.

4 Mauss' work on the gift raises a series of problems or ambiguities. As Osteen (2002b: 14) points out, contemporary treatments of the gift revolve around problems of 'freedom and autonomy, calculation and spontaneity, gratitude and generosity, risk and power'. Scholars have critiqued and developed Mauss' theorization of the gift in numerous ways.

Some examples include: Lévi-Strauss (1987) who suggests Mauss substitutes the parts of gift exchange for the whole, and as a result fails to understand the gift economy in its entirety (see Kaufman 2001); Bataille (1988–91) who uses Mauss' notion of the 'potlatch' to develop a theory of 'general economy' where excess is celebrated through wilful destruction, sacrifice and waste. His 'general economy' contrasts with the capitalist 'restricted economy' that is governed by notions of scarcity and restraint; Derrida (1992c) questions how a gift can be given freely when it is also located within a nexus of social obligation and calculation of social gain. This leads him to suggest that the gift is 'the impossible'. In contrast to Derrida, Testart (1998) argues that there are gifts free from obligation, and also different kinds of obligation (see also Laidlaw 2002). For a comprehensive overview including a number of different definitions of the gift, see Osteen (2002b: 2–37). See also Bourdieu (1977); Gregory (1982); Hyde (1983); Cheal (1988); Weiner (1992); Schrift (1997); Komter (1996); James and Allen (1998); Cullenberg *et al.* (2001).

5 Gregory's theories have been widely critiqued. See, for example, Mirowski (2001: 445), who disputes the circular nature of Gregory's distinction; Frow (1997: 102–30) who discusses the notion of inalienability, and the difference between gift and commodity exchanges; see also Laidlaw (2002).

6 For our purposes we rely on Gregory's analysis, however we are aware that this is the source of a contentious debate. Gregory views gift exchange and commodity exchange as diametrically opposed; Mirowski makes a distinction between the 'gift' and 'exchange' but suggests they are mutually dependent. He states 'gifts are an attempt to transcend the system of value; but in that system transcendence already presupposes some form of monetary structure. Without money . . . there is no "outside" to which to escape' (2001: 453–4). For a critique of Mirowski see Callari (2002).

4 The libidinal economy

> "What!" exclaimed the Ghost, "would you so soon put out, with worldly hands, the light I give? Is it not enough that you are of those whose passions made this cap, and force me through whole trains of years to wear it low upon my brow!"
> Scrooge reverently disclaimed all intention to offend, or any knowledge of having wilfully "bonneted" the Spirit at any period of his life. He made bold to inquire what business brought him there.
> "Your welfare!" said the Ghost.
>
> (Dickens, *A Christmas Carol*, [1843] 2003: 56)

The Ghost of Christmas Past takes Scrooge on a journey from childhood to adulthood in order to show him what he has relinquished for the sake of financial gain. This encounter suggests that his pursuit of wealth has come at a heavy price. The accumulation of economic riches has been accompanied by an impoverishment of those things without economic value: the social, the imaginative and the ethical. The Ghost exhorts Scrooge to remember, but what it shows him is painful. At the end of Stave Two of *A Christmas Carol*, Scrooge demands he be haunted no longer and extinguishes the Ghost's light with his cap. Before this happens, however, the reader glimpses the changes that will be effected by the visitations of the three ghosts over the course of the narrative.

Among 'the shadows of things that have been' (Dickens [1843] 2003: 68) illuminated by the spectre's light is a vision of Scrooge as a lonely schoolboy sitting reading. There is considerable pathos in this image, but Scrooge is not entirely alone. He is accompanied by literary figures conjured by his own imagination, among them characters from the *Thousand and One Nights* and *Robinson Crusoe*. He both observes and relives this boyhood moment in which Ali Baba and Robinson Crusoe appear to be as vividly real as Scrooge himself, and life and literary narrative come together to invoke the power of memory and mourning. In this moment, Scrooge is both 'actor and audience'. Further, 'It is the fusion of past and present which creates the emotional effect the story is aiming at' (Cerny 1997–98: 264). Indeed, both the Ghost of Christmas Past and literary imagination 'exceed [the] binary logic' of actor and audience, past and present. In this sense, they represent the 'experience of the impossible' (Derrida 1994: 63, 65, see also Chapter 2, this volume). Scrooge feels a pang of conscience for the boy he has turned away from his door the previous evening. He feels empathy for another and in this respect the text and the ghost are political – not political in the conventional sense or as revolution, but as a sense of responsibility and justice. In *Specters of Marx* (1994), the logic of spectrality is linked to contestations over the socio-economic (as indicated in the Foreshadowing, this volume), and this, too, is the purpose of Dickens' ghosts and his narrative.

The literary allusions in *A Christmas Carol* disrupt a further binary logic, the distinction between objective reality and narrative reality. The intertexts are not simply references to other works of fiction, but also entities with aesthetic and philosophical reality that precede and exist outside Dickens' text. Robinson Crusoe exists and yet does not, provoking the experience of the impossible for the reader. In this respect, it could be said that literature is also a medium in which the undecidability symbolized by the ghost is invoked. Indeed, we might go further to suggest that the arts broadly defined – literature, music, visual arts, theatre, cinema and so on – expand 'possibilities for thought and imagination, including ... the possibility of what it may be impossible to think or imagine' (Lucy 2004: 16). These possibilities and their political potential, we suggest, emerge in the *différance* (see also Chapter 2) between empirical reality and symbolic or narrative reality, fact and fiction, and the discourses of art, science and economy.

The French philosopher Jean-François Lyotard also attributes a political and philosophical role to aesthetic acts and experience. Like Derrida, Lyotard's notion of the political goes beyond institutional politics, and 'stands for all forms of action linked to change, or resistance to change' (Williams 1998: 3). And just as Derrida's hauntology supposes a relation between the experience of undecidability and the ethico-political decision, Lyotard believes that the political act is driven 'by feelings and desires that are sensitive to, and attracted to, events beyond understanding' (ibid.: 101). The undecidability that the spectre evokes is paralleled in Lyotard by the *differend*, a conflict which he explains in terms of incommensurability. When Lyotard refers to incommensurability, he means that different language games or genres, art and science for instance, share no common measure for judging or interpreting an event. The *differend* is the term he uses for the conflict that occurs when two language games come into dispute over the same event. Under these circumstances, the conflict cannot be satisfactorily resolved with justice to both, and in Lyotard's view it is the task of art, in particular the avant-garde, to bear witness to the *differend* or the twin faces of the conflict.

Avant-garde art forms break with tradition and existing norms. Drawing on Lyotard, Williams (ibid.: 109) explains, 'The avant-garde is the key to the necessary suspension of established forms of judgement and understanding' and it is the novelty of its expression which allows it to bear witness to the heterogeneity of the *differend*. As we will argue, the innovation that the avant-garde supposes is qualitatively different from innovation in the knowledge economy, above all, because it is political in the sense of responsibility, justice and resistance. According to Williams (ibid.: 110), the avant-garde '"dismantles consciousness" and "exceeds understanding" and yet it captures our attention through our feelings: something new must be thought through here'. It is 'the feeling associated with an event' – the sublime – 'which brings with it the impulse to act and the feeling that no action is the correct one' (ibid.: 103). This, too, is the function of hauntology.

The knowledge economy conceals the heterogeneity of the *differend* and the incommensurability of economic, social, cultural, aesthetic and scientific knowledge genres. It does so 'by subjecting any conflict or dispute to the test of profitability. The economic genre asks: which solution to the conflict makes economic sense?' (ibid.: 127). This leads us to ask, what role is there for knowledge which is incommensurate with the knowledge economy's economic logic and its handmaidens science and technology? Will the arts continue to fulfil the political and philosophical function both Lyotard and Derrida attribute to it, or will the knowledge economy seek to extinguish the illumination it provides, just as Scrooge did the ghost's light? To answer these questions, we bring Lyotard's postmodern theory together with his earlier work, *The Libidinal Economy* (first published 1974). A libidinal economy underlies the knowledge economy, in the same way as the unconscious underlies the conscious mind and haunting accompanies hegemony. How do the libidinal energies haunt the knowledge economy?

Libidinal economics in the knowledge economy

The libidinal economy is a philosophy of the economy of desire, a repudiation of Lyotard's earlier links with Marx's economic dialectics through its synthesis with Freud's psychoanalysis. Freud's notion of libidinal energy is an instinctual force.[1] The unconscious workings of desire cannot be rationalized or controlled by the Ego and are repressed in the process of psychological maturation and socialization. Desires, or what Lyotard (1993: xiii) calls 'intensities', are free-flowing impulses 'characterized by their displaceability' and resistance to closure, which return from the repressed and rupture the stability of conscious organizations. The unconscious is 'what is there and yet is hidden ... a blank space in a visible text' (Foucault 1973: 374), and Lyotard 'uses the premises of psychoanalytic thought to point to "a blank space" in the "visible text" of economic discourse' (Cooper and Murphy 1999: 239).

In *The Libidinal Economy*, Lyotard uncovers the hidden libidinal desires and affects in Marx's discourse. The surface discourse of politics and economy conceals 'those intensities which haunt Marx's thought' (Lyotard 1993: 104) – the desire to overthrow capitalism and commodity fetishism and to postpone their overthrow. It is in the incommensurability of closure and deferral, captivation and contempt, social concern and self-interest that Marx's desire emerges. This incommensurability parallels that of Freud's drives, Eros (the life drive) and Thanatos (the death drive). According to Readings' (1991: 103, original emphasis) interpretation, Lyotard understands Eros and Thanatos not as drives 'so much as two regimes which are not *opposed* but always co-present in their heterogeneity' and it is their incommensurability which constitutes desire. Lyotard brings these observations to bear not only on Marx the thinker, but political economy itself.

Lyotard describes capital as a 'disposition' or social structure that shares similarities with the Ego or consciousness insofar as its function is to modulate and moderate, repress and exploit libidinal energies.[2] It is the Ego which brings 'reason, order, logic, and social acceptability to the otherwise uncontrolled and potentially harmful biological drives' (Rivkin and Ryan 2004: 391), but it cannot fully control them. Lyotard identifies a comparable operation of desire and instinctual drives in capitalism:

> In simple terms, the entrepreneurial side of the capitalist economic system, or Capital, sees the energy of each feeling or desire as an opportunity, as something to be exploited. But the regulative, systematic, side of Capital needs to bring these individual desires and feelings into the system, through the power of comparison of monetary value. Therefore, Capital has a death drive, the drive to bend everything to a common measure, and an Eros, the drive to move into novel zones, to discover new opportunities.
>
> (Williams 1998: 60)

Clearly, there are parallels here with the economic principle of creative destruction, its function in the innovation process and thus economic growth in knowledge economies (see Chapter 2). There are further parallels between the policy rhetoric accompanying the innovation mantra – for instance, the imperative to 'generate, harness and exploit the creative power' (Department of Trade and Industry (UK) 2000) – and 'the drive to move into novel zones, to discover new opportunities'. The preeminence of innovation in knowledge economy policy takes capitalism's exploitation of creation and destruction and its harnessing of Eros and Thanatos and, thus, of libidinal energies, to a new level.

However, just as the conscious mind represses unruly drives, capitalism's very structure 'dissimulates', or covers over, impulsive libidinal intensities. It controls unstable energy through the systematic circulation of production, distribution, consumption and exchange. Williams believes Lyotard's notion of 'dissimulation' is the central concept of *The Libidinal Economy*, explaining it as 'the way in which a system always conceals within itself affects and hence other systems that are inconsistent with it and with each other' (2000: 40). In other words, the notion of 'dissimulation' draws attention to the fact 'that capitalism is supported by precisely the libidinal irrational intensities that it exists to regulate and exclude' (Readings 1991: 98). It does this through monetary equivalences. In capitalism, the notion of exchange-value (the value of a commodity in its exchange) demonstrates:

> the rate and ratio at which, at a given moment in time, one commodity exchanges with another; that is, its 'equivalence' in other commodities. Typically this expression of commodity equivalences is mediated through the money system and becomes apparent in the commodity's price. A commodity's price, therefore, does not reflect some intrinsic economic worth but rather is simply the abstracted expression of its exchange rate with other commodities which also bear their own price.
>
> (Lee 2000: xii)

Therefore, the laws of equivalence and exchangeability regulate the force of the desires capitalism recruits. However, to the extent that systemic regulation is incomplete, intensities and desires remain unpredictable, liable to eruption and destabilization. And, thus, the repressed ghost returns.

In our view, knowledge economy policy functions to regulate the exchange value of particular types of knowledge. The knowledge economy rationalizes and regulates knowledge in a number of different ways. First, knowledge is made commensurable – measured according to a common scale – in terms of its commodity exchange value. Second, as the privileged valuable commodity in the knowledge economy is scientific and technological knowledge, 'creativity' is strictly defined in terms of scientific and technological 'innovation'. Third, as technological innovation drives the knowledge economy, knowledge is further standardized, codified or digitalized as it is transmitted via ICTs. Any kind of knowledge and innovation that cannot be measured by the knowledge economy's standards (based on techno-efficiency and geared towards profit) remains neglected within this system. As Lyotard (1984: 4) asserts, 'knowledge is and will be produced in order to be sold, it is and will be consumed in order to be valorized in a new production: in both cases, the goal is exchange'. This means that knowledge must 'be operational (that is, commensurable) or disappear' (ibid. 1984: xxiv).

When knowledge economy policies define worthwhile knowledge, they exclude knowledge deemed marginal to current thinking about economic growth. They legitimate particular kinds of knowledge, specifically scientific and technological knowledge, whilst ignoring and diminishing others. Typically, cultural and aesthetic economies – thus, by implication, the arts and the political potential associated with them – have been regarded as incommensurable with the dominant techno-economic paradigm. This is marked by their absence in the literature through which we traced the evolution of the knowledge economy in Chapter 1. The arts have been perceived as less amenable than science and technology to the logic of the commodity and the regulatory systems we have described. Their impact and use-value is difficult to quantify. How can they be reproduced, standardized and normalized in ways that increase the rate of innovation and so economic growth (see also Chapter 1)?

Lyotard believes capitalism is driven by efficiency. Production and consumption are continually made cheaper and quicker so as to maximise the potential for profit. Knowledge and research and development in contemporary societies are driven by capitalism. Lyotard says that:

> capitalism has been able to subordinate to itself the infinite desire for knowledge that animates the sciences and to submit its achievements to its own criterion of technicity: the rules of performance that requires the endless optimization of the cost/benefit ratio.
>
> (1993: 25)

In the knowledge economy, the arts must also submit their achievements to capitalism's criterion of technicity or disappear. It is because of this perceived danger that capitalism is able to harness and exploit the libidinal or creative energies created by the incommensurability of such knowledge within the techno-economic discourse of the knowledge economy. What this means is that the market is permitted to define the rules, norms and values of these knowledge traditions. In the following section, we elaborate on the operations of this process in relation to the transformation of the arts into what have become known as the 'creative industries'.

The rise of the creative industries

> We need to keep pushing and trying to get people to be creative, because you won't advance if you're not creative. But that requires a bit of a mind shift in how you educate people to be creative.
>
> (Senior staff member, International Relations and Collaboration branch, Department of Education, Science and Training (Australian Commonwealth Government))

In 1997 the UK government established a Creative Industries Task Force, and the newly-created Department of Culture, Media and Sport (DCMS) prepared the *Creative Industries Mapping Document* (1998: online) in the following year. Here, and in the later 2001 *Mapping Document*, creative industries were defined as 'those activities which have their origin in individual creativity, skill and talent and which have the potential for wealth and job creation through the generation and exploitation of intellectual property' (DCMS 2001: online). In mapping the creative industries sector, it included what Hesmondhalgh (2002) regards as the core 'cultural' industries – Advertising, Film, Interactive Leisure Software, Music, Television and Radio, Performing Arts, Publishing and Software – and, in addition, Architecture, Arts and Antique Markets, Crafts, Design, and Designer Fashion.

In so doing, it recognized the existence of a creative economy, effectively moving the creative industries 'from the fringes to the mainstream' (Smith 1998: 9) and into the orbit of the knowledge economy.

The UK creative industries strategy is generally considered to be the prototype for contemporary creative industries policy frameworks and initiatives. Following the UK's lead, New Zealand Prime Minister Helen Clark identified the 'creative industries' as one of the target areas for enterprise and growth in the New Zealand economy. In Singapore, the Ministry of Information, Communication and the Arts spearheaded a creative industries strategy as part of its shift away from manufacturing and service, recognizing them to be 'one of the vanguards of economic growth' (MICA 2005: online). In Australia, by contrast, the creative economy has struggled to find its feet and the Australian Government's ongoing 'neglect' of the arts is demonstrated by its inability to incorporate 'culture and creativity into its national innovation agenda' (Seares 2001: 4). At the time of writing, the arts remained incidental to the country's national research priorities and it was only in 2005 that the first non-science Centre of Research Excellence was funded by the Australian Research Council (ARC). The ARC Centre of Excellence in Cultural and Media Industries is the successful outcome of sustained work by Stuart Cunningham (Director, Creative Industries Research Applications Centre) and John Hartley (Dean, Creative Industries Faculty) and their colleagues at the Queensland University of Technology (QUT). At the forefront of the creative industries push in Australia, Cunningham and Hartley also established the first federally-funded Cooperative Research Centre (CRC) for arts-based research. Their research publications describing the conceptual principles of their undertaking reveal much about the terms and conditions upon which the arts have entered the knowledge economy, and we draw on them here.

Cunningham and Hartley (2001: 7) believe that the Australian government's national innovation policy is limited by what they see as a 'commonsense' that '"creativity" means "scientists thinking creatively about innovation"'. This perception is arguably a consequence of innovation understood in terms of the techno-economic paradigm (see Chapter 2). Cunningham and Hartley's contention is reflected in broader discourses about creativity in the knowledge economy (see, for example, Caves 2000; Florida 2003; Howkins 2001; Leadbeater 1999). Although Howkins does not make the distinction explicit in his book, *The Creative Economy* (2001), he has since argued that there is a big distinction between innovation and creativity. In an interview, he says:

> Creativity is in the individual and it is subjective; innovation is group-based and is objective. Innovation always goes to a Committee at some stage and will only be allowed to continue if it is approved, whereas creativity is much more fuzzy and subjective. Creativity can move to

> innovation; creativity can power innovation; creativity can result in innovation. Innovation never causes creativity.
>
> (Ghelfi 2005: online)

Creativity of this sort has arguably always had legitimacy in the arts. However, what gives creativity legitimacy in the knowledge economy remains innovation, that is, a capacity for application (see Chapter 2) or ownership via intellectual property (see Chapters 3 and 5). The distinction between creativity and innovation is moot if, as Hartley argues, 'In the knowledge-driven economy, innovation becomes the means for wealth-creation. In this context creativity by itself has no value until it has a use, and the classic ... way to test usefulness is via market forces' (2004: xi).

Given this, the aim of the QUT initiative has been to disconnect technology and economy from the monopoly of science and reapply it to the creative industries so as to position them as drivers of new technologies and economic growth. The QUT enterprise 'provides one example of how research in the social and creative disciplines can be meaningfully hybridized with basic research in technology, to create new commercial opportunities' (Hartley *et al.* 2002: 1). It is an undertaking which shows that the arts, too, can follow the logic of commodity, technology and economy. In Hartley's (2004: xiii) view, although this alters the purpose and function of creative knowledge as it is conventionally understood, 'it may still sustain public, critical, even utopian, ambitions'.

As we have explained, dissimulation is central to the libidinal economy. Dissimulation potentially allows subversion from within the capitalist system. If Lyotard regards capitalism as the system best suited to regulating libidinal intensities, this does not mean to say that it is itself free of them or that other systems cannot play at the same game, 'a [form of] double dealing where each ... hides what it owes to the other' (Williams 1998: 92). In framing art as a discourse of commodity and technology, the creative industries are themselves engaged in a process of dissimulation, concealing the social, political, philosophical and critical aspects of creativity because they are inconsistent with the capitalist disposition. Dissimulation has political potential if that politics is understood as working with and against the system, disturbing consensus from within and making possible the emergence of new forms and new voices. The creative industries allow this potential and, as well, provide a means of ensuring that knowledge in the arts is recognized and valued. However, in our view there are a number of significant reasons why this is problematic, for the university and independent creative sectors in particular.

The *Creative Industries Mapping Document* (DCMS 1998: online) identified a range of applied arts which were in effect already industries, albeit overlooked in knowledge economy policy. It includes publishing but not literary studies, arts and antique markets, but not fine arts. However, given that such disciplines can be understood as providing theoretical, historical and critical resources that sustain the applied arts, the creative industries suggest themselves as a way of preserving such disciplines in an environment which privileges science and technology. Equally, however, they also threaten to absorb or diminish traditional arts disciplines. The argument that the creative arts must be 'reconceptualised in line with the realities of contemporary commercial democracies' (Cunningham 2001: 3) is not directed at policy-makers, but at the academy. It is not directed at the applied arts, but at the arts and humanities disciplines more broadly and at their failure to see themselves 'as part of the knowledge-based economy and as an integral and arguably central part of any decent innovation/R&D agenda, and to begin to win some degree of recognition for this association' (Cunningham 2002: 7).

This involves a reassessment of the purpose and role of the arts. One answer to their own rhetorical question 'What are the arts and humanities for?' is, the provision and 'analysis of code and content in the new economy' (Cunningham and Hartley 2001: 1). While they argue that the emphasis is on content, not its technological codification, 'content' is characteristically defined as information disseminated via the Internet, radio, television, advertising and the print media. QUT has a particular interest in areas such as human-computer interaction, user-interface design, network capacity, and new 'content growth areas' including 'online education, interactive television, multi-platform entertainment, computer games, and web design for business-to-consumer applications' (Cunningham 2002: 3). In this way, the creative industries align themselves with the key growth sectors in the science and technology sector.

The case for the creative industries is not presented as simply a matter of reframing those segments of the arts in ways which make their capacity to contribute to the knowledge economy transparent. It is informed by the assumption that the imperative to respond to the dominant techno-economic discourse has provided the catalyst for much needed change in the arts. This may mean that disciplinary knowledge that is incommensurate with technology becomes obsolete if, as Cunningham (ibid.: 9) asserts, 'We can no longer afford to understand the social and creative disciplines as commercially irrelevant, merely "civilising" activities.' In other words, the worth of arts disciplines can no longer be measured by their cultural or social function, whereby 'their value derives solely from public good arguments' (Hartley *et al.* 2002: 5). Moreover,

> By bringing the arts into direct contact with large-scale industries such as media entertainment, it allows us to get away from the elite/mass, art/entertainment, sponsored/commercial, high/trivial distinctions that bedevil thinking about creativity, not least in the old humanities.
>
> (Cunningham and Hartley 2001: 2)

At stake in these old dualisms is the idea of civic humanism, and the assumption that if it inheres in the fine arts, public culture and the academy, it is absent in the applied arts, popular culture and commerce (see Fahey *et al.* 2006). Artistic creativity, Cunningham and Hartley (2001: 3) argue, needs to be understood as 'something intrinsic, not opposed, to the productive capacities of a contemporary global, mediated, technology-supported economy'. In our view, however, the 'democratization' of the creative arts and humanities simply replaces competing ideological assumptions with a single one, the ideology of the market. As we will show, this substantially alters the way in which artistic work is created and received, produced and consumed. It also alters our understanding of the critical, political, and aesthetic function of art in its own right and as an object of academic inquiry.

The applied arts – advertising, fashion, media, design and so forth – are intrinsic to the market. Artistic creativity in this context is arguably channelled into the impersonal manufacture of 'an impersonal commodity' for a mass consumption (McDonald 1957: 59). As Lyotard (1993: 251) puts it, 'repetition is primary since it is included in the very constitution of the element: concept, commodity. If it is not repeatable, equally exchangeable, it is not an element of the system'. This raises the distinction between high art and mass art to which Cunningham and Hartley allude.

There is a vast literature debating this matter which we cannot address here. That said, the creative arts more broadly have long existed 'within larger psycho-political-economic-cultural frameworks' (Wilson 2002: 6). Indeed, in 1936 Adorno wrote to Walter Benjamin stating that both high art and mass-produced art 'bear the stigmata of capitalism' (quoted in Bernstein 1991: 2) and that they effectively represent a division of labour. At the same time, they represent two possibilities for social transformation. The one is not intrinsically better or worse than the other – Dickens produced many of his novels in serial form for mass consumption. Rather, Adorno believed that the division between both forms of art is imposed from outside through a process of reification which has its origins in Enlightenment reason. He saw high art and the 'culture industries' as two halves which do not make a whole, thus suggesting that the 'potentialities of culture for radical transformation are themselves divided, torn' (ibid.: 3).

But will the so-called democratization of the arts implied in QUT's creative industries project necessarily bridge the high/low divide? Bernstein's (1991: 6) explanation of the political difference between high art and mass art reveals something of the dissimulation which operates in any disposition:

> High art is bought at the price of the exclusion of the lower classes – 'with whose cause, the real universality, art keeps faith precisely by its freedom from the ends of the false universality' [Horkheimer and Adorno 1973: 135]. Illusory universality is the universality of the art of the culture industry, it is the universality of the homogenous same, an art that no longer even promises happiness but only provides the easy entertainment as relief from labour.

In Adorno's view, then, the culture industries are an instrument whereby leisure is co-opted by capital, presenting 'culture as the realization of the right of all to the gratification of desire while in reality continuing the negative integration of society' (Bernstein 1991: 3). McDonald (1957: 60) makes a similar point when he claims that mass culture 'is manufactured for mass consumption by technicians employed by the ruling class and it is not an expression of either the individual artist or the common people'. He suggests that state propaganda or pedagogy is no different from entertainment mass culture since each 'exploits rather than satisfies the cultural needs of the masses'. The only difference is that the state exploits 'for political rather than commercial reasons' (ibid.).

The intensification of the alignment of artistic creativity with economic enterprise in the knowledge economy is as much political as economic insofar as it is legitimated by the policy rhetoric to which it responds. As a consequence, 'notions of "creativity" and "innovation", catch-cries in the construction of a knowledge economy, move away from "imagination", "invention" and "intervention" as the arts undergo a political reconfiguration' (Grierson 2003: 5). As the arts and humanities remake themselves in the service of the creative industries, they position themselves not as critics, commentators and theorists of the cultural economy, but to exploit the libidinal energies which Lyotard says capitalism is so well-placed to regulate.

Mass consumer culture – including mass art – is a libidinal economy in which social and market structures and dispositions release, channel and exploit desires and feelings – those intensities that sustain and subvert it (see Kenway and Bullen 2005). The primary operation of capitalism is commodification and, therefore, it is a disposition which controls the energy of intensities through the logic of the commodity. Thus, while the emphasis in the creative industries is ostensibly on production, consumer desire is critical. One of the central tenets of consumer capitalism and the culture it promotes is desire for

> an extensive range of commodities, goods and experiences which are to be consumed, maintained, planned and dreamt about by the general population. Yet this consumption is far from being just the consumption of utilities which are addressed to fixed needs. ... Rather, consumer culture through advertising, the media, and techniques of display of goods, is able to destabilize the original notion of use or meaning of goods and attach to them new images and signs which can summon up a whole range of associated feelings and desires.
>
> (Featherstone 1992: 114)

In other words, consumer capitalism encompasses a shift which the knowledge economy largely conceals, a shift in focus 'from production to selling, from the satisfaction of stable needs to the "invention" of new desires'

(Humphery 1998: 25). The knowledge economy is arguably consumption-driven – according to Hartley *et al.* (2002: 1), 60–70 per cent of GDP – and the creative industries are one of the fastest growing sectors in the global economy (Rifkin 2000). The industry and commercial focus of the creative industries means they are able to contribute to this growth not only within, but also beyond the creative sector by supporting companies as they 'struggle to understand how to develop new business that is focused on the complexities of human desire' (Hartley *et al.* 2002: 8).

This focus on human desire shifts the locus of artistic creativity away from the personal expressivity of the individual artist to the consumer, and to how creativity can be co-opted to promote consumer desire and thus economic growth. This is the point where the commodity takes up secondary use-values and is determined by a wide range of cultural associations and illusions. Commodity fetishism regulates consumers' sense of satisfaction and dissatisfaction by binding consumption to pleasure and by redefining desire as a need that the individual seeks to fill through consumption. Indeed, we would go further to suggest that commodification of the creative arts exploits the desire of those with aspirations to artistic creativity. According to Angela McRobbie (2002: 517),

> The flamboyantly *auteur* relation to creative work that has long been the mark of being a writer, artist, film director or fashion designer is now extended to a much wider range of 'individuated' workforce. The media has glamorized creative individuals as uniquely talented 'stars'.

In McRobbie's view, the publication of the *Creative Industries Mapping Document* made the creative sector in the UK the object of 'intense commercial interest' which has substantially transformed the sector. A key issue is the fact that the 'small scale previously independent micro-economics of art and culture' (ibid.: 517) has been replaced by a neo-liberal model which privileges 'entrepreneurialism, individualization and reliance on commercial sponsorship' (ibid.) in ways that compromise creativity and the political culture. She points to a number of ways in which the desire for creative expression has been exploited, arguing that 'recent attempts by the large corporations to innovate in this sector mean that the independents are, in effect, dependent subcontracted suppliers' (ibid.: 523). These developments militate against public funding of the arts (see Chapter 3) while artists themselves are left with little opportunity for truly independent work or reflective and critical engagement with the cultural sphere: 'speed and risk negate ethics, community and politics' (ibid.). To what extent does education and training for the knowledge economy reinforce this?

Under the auspices of the creative industries, the role of higher education in disseminating knowledge is reoriented towards the vocational, commercial and technological. In contrast to a Bachelor of Arts, a Bachelor of Creative Industries 'prepares you to work as an entrepreneur in the global knowledge economy', enticing prospective students by maintaining it is at 'the forefront of entrepreneurial, cultural, commercial and creative developments' (QUT 2004). It is not only aesthetic knowledge and creation which needs to be understood as part of a 'whole product value proposition' (Hartley *et al.* 2002: 8), able to be reproduced, packaged and sold, but arts education. As a result, 'tertiary education is increasingly folded into the service of the industry-model with applied learning taking over from critical or "deep" learning' (Grierson 2003: 5). The consequent 'emphasis on skills and production' involves deskilling of another kind – a reduction in a deep intellectual engagement with an established body of disciplinary knowledge. It shifts the purpose of critical engagement from the political to the promotion of consumer desire.

The creative industries' response to the marginalization of creative knowledge in the knowledge economy shifts the arts and humanities centre of gravity towards the production of the aesthetic entrepreneur or, more broadly, a 'creative class' whose knowledge work involves the production and commodification of intensities. The rub is that consumer desire – and this includes the desire of the educational consumer – persists only as long as it remains unsatisfied. As a product is assimilated into the marketplace, it eventually generates less profit as its novelty and, thus, desirability diminishes. The result is product senility and aesthetic obsolescence, leading to the rapid turnover of style and fashion and the creation of an artificial sense of insufficiency. The expenditure of creative knowledge in the service of desire means that the arts, arts education and arts-based research (such as electronic game design), also operate according to a market logic of innovation and perforce obsolescence. In seeking to be commensurable with knowledge economy discourse, the creative industries and the disciplinary knowledge they encompass are subject to the economic logic of creative destruction and the libidinal logic of Eros and Thanatos. Inevitably, certain arts and disciplinary knowledge will perish. How will the creative industries attest to their ghosts?

Lyotard and the politics of art

> There's a bigger need for engineers and ICT related jobs, management etc than there is, let's say, for poets and English literature ... [but] if you want to educate citizens that are critical thinkers, all round thinkers, then it's not enough to only educate people for that specific market-pushed need. You create the gap in your society and who is going to take responsibility for that gap to be filled?
>
> (Senior staff member, UNESCO Forum on Higher Education, Research and Knowledge, Division of Higher Education)

Despite the totalizing discourse of the knowledge economy, a disposition that seeks to homogenize and regulate the field of knowledge according to the laws of equivalence and exchangeability, it still harbours its own contradictions that haunt the system from within. The very dependence of the creative industries on unpredictable libidinal energies means that they are liable to eruption. In the knowledge economy, creative knowledge need not be understood as being either 'opposed' or 'intrinsic' to this structure or disposition. Rather, from Lyotard's perspective, creative knowledge is an intensity that operates both 'within and against' (Readings 1991: 38) the knowledge economy. 'Dissimulation' is also 'a way of acting that undermines systems by ... releasing the energy that they exploit and capture' (Williams 1998: 102). On the one hand, the creative industries reframe creative knowledge in the interests of the knowledge economy, 'dissimulating' this 'intensity' by converting it into an exchangeable value through a process of both commodification and codification. On the other hand, there are also other forms of creative knowledge that retain their intensity within the knowledge economy, and make 'the system leak, setting it in movement towards new possibilities that demand a creative response' (Williams 2000: 44).

To be political, however, the arts must operate at the intersection of oppositional discourses. Lyotard insists that the political enters only when different spheres, different metanarratives, different knowledge systems, come into contact with one another: art and science, high art and mass art, for example. However, these are understood not in terms of dualities, but duplicity. Thus, unlike Adorno, who argues that the division between high art and mass culture divides the potential of culture to catalyse social transformation; unlike the creative industries which seek to make creativity commensurate with science and commerce, Lyotard's politics of art is generated at the point of incommensurability, where it can attest to the *differend*.

As we indicated earlier in this chapter, the revolutionary potential of art is most fully realized in the avant-garde. As Williams (1998: 6) explains:

> Here, the shock value and innovation of the work of art takes on a political significance as acts that disturb the status quo and force us to think anew. Artists can show the limits and flaws of set ways of thinking and acting. They can return us to more fundamental sensations that have been hidden under elaborate forms of thought.

As a movement, the avant-garde can be characterized as art which rejects the commodification of art, indeed 'reacts to the emergence of mass art by attempting to sustain the values of so-called high art, most notably the value of personal expression' (Carroll 1998: 18). In a more general sense, the avant-garde should be understood as an aesthetic and an ethos which is at odds with the way in which innovation is conceived in the knowledge economy. Some examples illustrate this point.

Andreas Gursky is a contemporary German artist who uses photography precisely for the purposes of critiquing commodity capitalism.[3] We suggest that Gursky's photography is high art, not opposed to, but *as* mass art. This is both literally and metaphorically the case. His images are overwhelming in size, and they invariably depict mass gatherings of people on the crowded floor of the stock exchange, at rock concerts, or at rave parties. Photography is also a medium which can be endlessly reproduced. In terms of the latter point, parallels can be drawn between photography's endless reproducibility and the incessant repetition that is a primary characteristic of commodity capitalism and the mass consumer culture it promotes. Through his work, Gursky bears witness to the twin faces of capital, his politics is generated at the point of incommensurability, where he acknowledges the duplicity and, draws attention to the inherent contradictions within and excesses of commodity capitalism.

99 Cent (1999; see Figure 4.1) is a large-format (6 ft high and 11 ft wide), sharply focused image of a discount store in Los Angeles where there are endless rows of '99 cent' consumables (i.e. chocolate bars, sweets and caramels) on display. The literal 'equivalence' between these commodities creates a dilemma of sorts: if all the commodities are the same price then how does the consumer determine their intrinsic worth? If, as we suggest, commodity capitalism is driven by an insatiable desire to consume, then one possible answer to this question might be: 'by getting more for less'. Gursky explores this paradox visually by contrasting the massive scale of the photograph with the minimum price of the products, as everything is so cheap in the '99 cent' store you can afford to buy up big.

Lyotard suggests that in commodity capitalism 'repetition is primary' (1993: 251). However, as *99 Cent* shows, if you repeat something endlessly, all detail tends to blur into a uniformity of colour. The large-scale format of the photograph is in keeping with the excesses of the commercialized image-world of commodity culture. But the photograph also takes the seductive edge off these goods. The sheer size of the image reduces them to mere form, an abstract grid of undifferentiated commodities, 'a sequence repeated in goods, shelves and signs, as far as the eye can see' (Ohlin 2002: 25). Thus the image also suggests another contradiction within commodity culture: mass availability is predicated on consumer choice, and yet, when consumers are confronted with such an extensive variety of options, it becomes overwhelming, perhaps even impossible for them to decide.

Gursky's images of industrial interiors, German factories such as Mercedes, Grundig and Siemens, take the viewer to the site of capitalism's material conditions of production. According to Ohlin, 'being able to see exactly what is going on inside does not necessarily educate the viewer, or explain how political or economic systems actually work' (ibid.). However, in terms of Lyotard's notion of the libidinal economy, the horizontal rows of overhead lights and the vertical columns of pillars in *Siemens, Karlsruhe* (1991; see Figure 4.2) do create a visual matrix representing the ways in which the capitalist 'disposition' is structured upon order and control. Gursky may indeed present 'a highly superficial, aestheticized approach to the sites of labor' (Alberro 2001: 114), but it is precisely his aestheticization

Figure 4.1 *99 Cent* (1999), Andreas Gursky.

Figure 4.2 *Siemens, Karlsruhe* (1991), Andreas Gursky.

of seemingly banal industrial spaces that draws our critical attention to them, and 'forces us to think anew'.

Photography is also the medium for social and political critique in Christos Tsiolkas' *Dead Europe* (2005a). The narrator of the novel, a Greek-Australian photographer, Isaac, reflects on the nature of art, its commodification and the purpose of arts education when he renews his acquaintance with a friend from college. They debate the difference between Sal's 'real photography, the photos he is not paid to take' (ibid.: 203) and his work in pornography where beauty, art, aesthetics and ethics play no part. There is a disjunction between the photographic images, one set exploits, the other gives expression. This leads Isaac to remember his college experiences – his second-year lecturer whose 'skill was her knowledge, her craft her preparation, her passion, her drive to convince her students of the humanitarian basis of art . . . For her, art could only be democratic' (ibid.: 213). Isaac's own experience photographing unionized workers undercuts such idealistic visions of art – truth is not beauty. However, it is political. The more important theme in *Dead Europe* is contemporary capitalism in post-communist Europe. Tsiolkas' *Dead Europe* portrays a Europe haunted by the spectres of the past.

The ghostly boy who appears in Isaac's photos is a Jewish boy, murdered when left in the care of a young Greek peasant couple during the Second World War. He is a victim not so much of the Holocaust but of a combination of superstition, racism, fear and avarice. These are figured as irrational libidinal forces present in the twin narratives of the novel. The historical tale tells the story of the boy and the succeeding generations of the family who murdered him, including their migration to Australia, and concludes in present time. It thus informs the second, contemporary narrative. This follows Isaac's journey across Europe, from Athens to Prague, Venice to Paris, and Amsterdam to Cambridge and the barely repressed anti-Semitism he encounters.

The function of 'the Jews' in the text is problematic and Australian public intellectual Robert Manne (2005) argues that the novel teeters on the edge of anti-Semitism itself. Images of dispossession, capitalism, conspiracy and vengeance are indeed linked with 'the Jews', but also with post-communist Europe more broadly. Post-communist Europe is linked with what McQueen (2005: online) describes as 'the thriving of superstition in a world conducted – supposedly – in accord with the Weberian rationality of industry and science'. Hatred and superstition are libidinal energies which capital cannot regulate, suggesting that it perverts desire in seeking to control it. Thanatos, the death drive, pervades both of Tsiolkas' narratives, but most explicitly in the contemporary narrative. The reader is confronted with shocking images of explicit sex, violence, drugs and the horror of the protagonist's dissolution. Both mass and elite culture are emptied of meaning.

> Arsenal. Man United. Big Brother. Who wants to be a Millionaire? Lager. Stout. Arsenal ... Lager, Lager, Wine, Wine, Wine, mundane, haven't I seen it all before, she's becoming boring, her art's always been boring, Arsenal, Man United.
>
> (Tsiolkas 2005a: 364)

History is reduced to show and spectacle and, ultimately, Isaac, the cultural tourist is jaded. He cannot be bothered waiting in a queue to visit the Anne Frank Museum in Amsterdam; he can no longer be bothered to mourn.

As Derrida would have it, 'To avoid the being-there of the ghost is to avoid being true to justice' (Lucy 2004: 117). The ghost in Tsiolkas' novel represents the cost of forgetting. The triumph of capitalism is not the end of history. According to historian McQueen (2005: online), atavism is the 'soil for imagining *Dead Europe*. Capitalism might have beaten off the future, but it has yet to vanquish the past'. As such, the ghost in this narrative does not only ask us to mourn, but to look to the future for traces of a past that 'is never over' (ibid.). This is what we can infer when Rebecca, Isaac's mother, tells his lover, Colin:

> They will suffer again. She said this quietly. And as soon as she said it, she knew it to be true. Could he not see it? In just three days she had seen

> it. The beggars in the streets, the Slav girls who cleaned the toilets in the hotel, the train stations plastered with warnings of terror. Their fear, their anxiety, it suffused the city. Could Colin not see the truth of the photographs? Isaac had not photographed the past, he had captured the future. She could not wait to get home.
>
> (Tsiolkas 2005a: 405)

The ghost in this novel, therefore, is the spectral embodiment of a politics which emerges in the *différance* between, and therefore the interdependence of, past, present and future. Equally, we could say that *Dead Europe* brings together the incommensurable discourses of superstition and rationalism, the gratification of desire and the desire for justice, and in so doing bears witness to the *differend*. The novel is profoundly disturbing and often repellent, but what it expresses

> Has nothing to do with the *petit frisson*, the cheap thrill, profitable pathos, that accompanies innovation. ... Through innovation, the will affirms its hegemony over time. ... The avant-gardist task remains that of undoing the presumption of the mind with respect to time.
>
> (Lyotard 1989: 210–11)

As such, the novel 'is a testimony free of the possibility of resolution' (Williams 1998: 109), posing questions it does not answer. And yet at the same time *Dead Europe*, and indeed fiction *per se*, does function to open up a dialogue with/about ghosts, and as a means to engage with political issues. In a recent interview, Tsiolkas states:

> What fiction allowed me to do was offer a portrayal of Europe and the contemporary world that gave a spiritual and existential dimension of the historic moment we are living in. I believe fiction can do this and I think some of the greatest modern fiction has always done this. I want the reader to experience not only the contemporary Europe but the smells and sensuality and horror of the old peasant Europe as well.
>
> (2005b: online)

Tsiolkas' novel illustrates the benefits of talking to ghosts.

* * *

Derrida's *différance* and Lyotard's *differend* pose central questions for the knowledge economy. Can it tolerate, accommodate and nurture those forms of knowledge that are incommensurate with it, or must it capture and domesticate them through its economic logics of techno-efficiency and commodity exchange? Indeed, can it tame incommensurable knowledge? Through a discussion of the unruly ghost of the libidinal economy, we have answered these questions with regard to the arts.

Our argument has been that the ghost of the libidinal economy can be understood as the knowledge economy's unconscious. And, we suggested, the Ego, or in Lyotard's terms the 'disposition', of the knowledge economy seeks to control, channel and exploit its unconscious libidinal intensities. Our interest has been in the libidinal intensities of the arts; especially their political intensities. For as Derrida says, 'it is necessary to speak *of the* ghost ... from the moment that no ethics, no politics, whether revolutionary or not seems possible and thinkable' (1994: xix, original emphases).

The arts have typically been seen as incommensurate by the knowledge economy and thus of little use. Given the knowledge economy's hegemony this has evoked a sense of danger in the arts world, a fear of obliteration. The knowledge economy has preyed on this fear. As we have revealed with regard to the rise of the creative industries in certain policy circles and in the university sector, the knowledge economy has invited the arts to move into the hegemonic zone.

Some aspects of the arts, namely the creative industries, have accepted this invitation with alacrity, taking up a commensurate identity. The creative industries have thus, in a sense, become the Ego of the arts taking on the 'disposition' of the knowledge economy in the name of the creative economy. Further, they have proclaimed this as a desirable egalitarian move which takes the arts beyond the traditional constraining binaries of the 'culture industries'; a move, they suggest, invokes Derrida's *différance*. But, we have argued, the creative industries' ascent into the hegemonic zone has largely locked them into the highly restrictive logics of the commodity and consumerism. This move has also excluded them from the political and critical politics of Lyotard's *differend*. In other words it has led them to repress the arts' libidinal ghosts.

However, not all libidinal intensities can be so readily conscripted. The libidinal is always liable to leak and, in many ways, the arts depend on the release of libidinal intensities; dissimulation is their life-blood. The politics of art, above all avant-garde art, occurs at the point of incommensurability between different genres: at the *differend*. Further, the libidinal economy is constituted in the *différance* between the will to harness and to liberate the arts. Derrida (1994: xviii, original emphases) maintains:

> What happens between the two, and between all the 'two's' one likes, such as between life and death, can only *maintain itself* with some ghost, can only *talk with or about* some ghost. So it would be necessary to learn spirits. Even and especially if this, the spectral, *is not*.

Notes

1 According to Barry (2002: 97), the libido 'is the energy drive associated with sexual desire. In classic Freudian theory, it has three stages of focus, the *oral*, the *anal*, and the *phallic*. The libido in the individual is part of a more generalized drive

which the later Freud called *Eros* (the Greek work for "love"), which roughly means the life instinct, the opposite of which is *Thanatos* (the Greek word for "death") which roughly means the death instinct' (original emphases).

2 It should be noted that while Lyotard considers the capitalist economy as overarching, there are many different kinds of dispositions which channel libidinal energies. The sex and death drives are regulated by, among other things, the Church, family, legal system and education.

3 Gursky studied at the Kunstakademic in Dusseldorf in the 1980s. Hilla and Bernd Becher taught photography at this school in the 1950s and developed a form of photographic distance called 'impersonal objectivity': where shots of industrial architecture were systematically classified. Joseph Beuys was Professor of Sculpture at the school in the 1960s instructing artists such as Anselm Kiefer, Sigmar Polke and Gerhard Richer. It is this rich artistic tradition that informs and influences Gursky's work.

5 The survival economy

> "Mercy!" he said. "Dreadful apparition, why do you trouble me?"
> "Man of the worldly mind!" replied the Ghost, "do you believe in me or not?"
> "I do," said Scrooge. "I must. But why do spirits walk the earth, and why do they come to me?"
> "It is required of every man," the Ghost returned, "that the spirit within him should walk abroad among his fellow-men, and travel far and wide; and if that spirit goes not forth in life, it is condemned to do so after death. It is doomed to wander throughout the world – oh, woe is me! – and witness what it cannot share, but might have shared on earth, and turned to happiness!"
> (Dickens, *A Christmas Carol*, [1843] 2003: 47)

Scrooge understands himself as a 'man of the worldly mind' until he is confronted by the problems of the way he has lived his life and of his possible ghostly and ghastly living-on: a doomed wandering of regret about what he 'might have shared on earth, and turned to happiness'. He is faced with what Laclau (1995: 88), drawing on Derrida, says is a 'constitutive anachronism of identity'. 'Life,' Laclau argues, 'emerges out of a more basic life/death dichotomy – it is not "life" as uncontaminated presence but *survie* [living-on] that is the condition of any presence' (ibid.). Scrooge's 'spirit' has not gone 'forth in life'. Further, he has lived his life as an 'uncontaminated presence' and has ignored his own and others' 'living on'. He has shown no 'respect for those others who are no longer or for those others who are not yet *there* ... whether they are already dead or not yet born' (Derrida 1994: xix, original emphasis).

Those who are 'no longer', nonetheless invoke 'the persistence of a present past, the return of the dead ... ' (ibid.: 101). They have what Derrida calls 'living subjectivity' which 'can, itself, speak and speak of itself, leave traces or legacies beyond the living present of its life' (ibid.: 187). There is a particular poignancy associated with the traces or ghosts in the present of those 'who are no longer', but whose ways of life have previously been exploited or destroyed by men 'of the worldly mind': '[b]e they victims of wars, political or other kinds of violence, nationalist, racist, colonialist, sexist, or other kinds of exterminations, victims of the oppressions of capitalist imperialism or any of the forms of totalitarianism' (ibid.: xix). Their 'living on' invokes the ever-present possibility of the repetition in the present and the future of past practices of subjugation. Such repetition is all the more likely when the spectres of past injustices are repressed or denied and when haunting thus fades and forgetting transpires.

But, as Derrida announces and as Scrooge finds to his great discomfort, 'a ghost never dies, it remains always to come and to come-back' (ibid.: 99). Of 'spirits', Derrida says, '*one must* reckon with them' (ibid.: xx, original emphasis). When the forgotten or repressed revenant returns, it not only problematizes the lines 'between the living and the non-living', it also shows 'that the seeming priority of life in fact presupposes a *sur-vie* that undermines this priority' (Critchley 1995: 10). In other words, a focus on the present, and those living in the present, is given priority over the past and the future. But *sur-vie* challenges this priority. In turn, this invokes

> the principle of some *responsibility*, beyond all living present, within that which disjoins the living present, before the ghosts of those who are not yet born or who are already dead.
>
> (Derrida 1994: xix, original emphasis)

The ghostly visitation experienced by Scrooge is an invitation to responsibility and justice. Indeed, when Dickens speaks of ghosts, he does so in the name of responsibility to the past, present and future. For Derrida, such a 'spectral moment' includes a complex notion of the future which he calls the 'to come' (Derrida 1994: xx). Although for Derrida the future will always be 'to come', it nonetheless 'is also the condition of possibility for change in the present' (Patton 2004: 34). The 'to come' does not reproduce or repeat the present. Rather it is more like a promise which 'in relation to some future state of affairs has consequences for one's actions in the present' (ibid.: 24).

Survival economies haunt the knowledge economy and when we speak of its ghosts in this chapter, we do so in the name of responsibility and justice to the past, the present and the future. We begin with a description of the distinctive aspects of survival economies, briefly comparing them with market economies and identifying their particular relationship to knowledge and nature. We then note some ways that they have been, and continue to be, exploited and depleted. Our focus here is on certain current repetitions of subjugation in relation to the knowledge economy, namely the exploitative practices and politics associated with bio-prospecting, patenting nature, and trade related intellectual property rights. This is followed by a discussion of the manner in which indigenous knowledge activists respond to the threat of such subjugation by invoking the 'spectral moment'. With a particular focus on debates about biopiracy and its consequences, we consider the knowledge claims upon which such resistance is justified and some issues associated with various approaches to amelioration. We conclude with a discussion of the broad parameters of the knowledge that survival economies offer the planet about the 'to come'. Our major source is Vandana Shiva, a world-renowned ecology and economics thinker and activist from India whose work over recent decades has been widely influential in shaping counter-hegemonic opinion on the global knowledge politics of ecology, economics and justice (Shiva *et al.* 1991; Shiva 1993, 1997, 1999, 2000a, 2000b, 2000c, 2004, 2005).

Survival economies and indigenous knowledge

> It's more than new technology. It's local knowledge, it's something which is created in a community, which is needed by communities to solve problems, a community's way of handling problems. They may or may not use new technology. They may use other technologies. This is how people need to live their lives, how they need to survive.
>
> (Senior staff member, Communications and Information Section, UNESCO)

What are 'survival economies' and what is their relationship to knowledge and nature? The concept 'survival economies' is occasionally employed to refer to 'traditional subsistence' economies marked by economies of shortage or lack (Neef 2002; Aritho 2001) and as ripe for economic change (Hart 1997; Hart and Milstein 1999). However, Shiva, with others, introduced a more robust and positive construction of the term in a report to the United Nations University's programme on Peace and Global Transformations. In this report titled *Ecology and the Politics of Survival: conflicts over natural resources in India*, Shiva *et al.* (1991) produce a powerful conceptual framework for evaluating modern economic development from an ecological perspective and, more particularly, for analysing the connections between economic development and conflicts over natural resources. Via this framework, they seek to address the 'incompetence' of modern economics in dealing with natural resources. They say that 'the elevation of the market to the position of the highest organising principle of society led to the neglect of the other two vital economies in development thought' (ibid.: 29).

These two other economies are 'the economy of natural ecological processes' (nature's economy) and the 'survival economy'. Of the former, they explain: 'Natural resources are produced and reproduced through a complex network of ecological processes' (ibid.: 30). Production, such as the 'production of humus by forests and the regeneration of water resources', is integral to this economy. The survival economy, they argue, 'has given human societies the material basis of survival by deriving livelihoods directly from nature through self-provisioning mechanisms' (ibid.: 31–2). Such economies are organized around the principles of sustenance and the satisfaction of basic needs and involve the direct utilization of common natural resources and a proper acknowledgement of the life support utility of such natural commons. Clearly, both economies are closely entwined.

Large numbers of rural people within the so-called Third World, predominantly farmers, herders and hunters, derive their livelihood from survival economies. Their survival is 'primarily dependent directly on the products of nature outside the market system' (ibid.: 15). The seed is the first 'link' in the food chain and the survival economy, and small-scale self-sufficient farmers, for example, save, swap, barter, or sell seeds to each other. They have 'selected, improved, evolved crops and seeds over the centuries, and created the tremendous diversity of crops and cultures that have nourished the world' (Shiva 2000a: 54). Survival economies have long demonstrated their practicability in contexts that are very different from the market economy. Indeed, Shiva argues across her many publications, such economies generate material wealth in ways that conflict with market economies. They have a different sense of relationships between people (sharing rather than enclosing, cooperative rather than competitive), between people and nature (in harmony with rather than exploitative of) and, overall, of what is required to sustain livelihood and life itself.

Survival economies have their own distinctive science and technology systems. Shiva challenges the commonsense equation of science and technology with modernity and Westernization. She views science as 'ways of knowing' and technology as 'ways of doing' and argues that all societies have science and technology systems on which their distinctive and divergent development has been based (1993: 135). She seeks to rescue survival economies from the modernist (industrial–scientific) notion that they are backward, stagnant, and primitive and involve low productivity. Unlike those who situate the survival economy in a developmental trajectory, and unlike many theorists of Third World development,[1] Shiva and her colleagues make the case that survival economies are associated with diverse systems of biological and other knowledge and diverse cultures. Indeed, biological diversity is understood as the material base of much cultural diversity. Ecology is seen as a basis for economy. Survival economies are not seen as unscientific but as subscribing to a different system of science and technology, which involves 'different criteria of choice or rationality that guides resource use patterns for human needs satisfaction' (Shiva *et al.* 1991: 39). This approach involves:

> A knowledge system with an ecological understanding of nature;
> A technological system for processing resources to satisfy human needs with minimum resources waste;
> Rationality criteria for demarcating vital and non-vital needs and between resource destructive and resource enhancing technologies.
>
> (Ibid.: 41)

Shiva *et al.* (ibid.) equate such views with 'indigenous science and technology systems' which, 'whether documented or orally held, are collective, cumulative and involve ongoing innovation'. These systems can, for instance, relate to a range of plants including crop species and healing plants.

Today, roughly 15 years after the publication of Shiva *et al.*'s landmark report, the indigenous science and technology systems of survival economies are often described as 'indigenous knowledge', 'traditional knowledge' or 'traditional ecological knowledge'.[2] In economic parlance, such science and technology systems are often understood as 'indigenous natural capital'. In this book we will use the term 'indigenous knowledge'. The US anthropologist Michael Brown describes indigenous knowledge as 'local lore drawing on centuries of observation and engagements with particular environments' (2003: 206). His book *Who Owns Native Culture?* (2003) is a richly researched, insightful and provocative study of the many issues associated with indigenous knowledge today, and we have found it an invaluable resource. In it, he also points to the links between biological diversity and cultural diversity and to the ways that these come together for indigenous peoples (ibid.: 133). For example, Brown (ibid.: 227–8), drawing on the anthropological research of Brody, tells of the Beaver Indians of British Columbia for whom 'land is a livelihood, a legacy and a moral community'. He contrasts this with the views of British Columbia's planners and entrepreneurs for whom, in this example at least, land is 'little more than a basket of resources to be analysed, parsed and consumed'. This is one of many similar case studies conducted in various countries around the world where different knowledges, cultures, and economies connect, collide, collude and eventually, and in various ways, and with various consequences, resolve their differences. As Brown demonstrates, each case study points to the current complexity of the issues involved, particularly in an increasingly mobile and hybridizing world, and to important political and ethical issues.

Subjugating the survival economy

> Knowledge always comes not from the top but from below. Maybe it becomes mainstream, it may be used by multinationals in order to be exploited. That's another problem of knowledge.
>
> (Senior staff member, Communication and Information Section, UNESCO)

In what ways have survival economies been exploited and depleted by market economies and, their most recent manifestation, knowledge economies? Plant and animal exchange has long been linked to the movement of peoples around the world for the purposes of exploration, trade, war, travel, resettlement and research. This is well documented, as are instances of 'reciprocal exchange' that have occurred in the process. However, the transfer of indigenous knowledge from survival economies to colonial market economies was a characteristic feature of colonialism and as such can be understood as occurring in a context of domination, deception and exploitation. For instance, Brown (2003: 106) tells of the manner in which the British first secured quinine, rubber and tea through specimens smuggled from Brazil and China and then cultivated industrial crops in the colonized countries of South East Asia, India and Ceylon. Such expansions of agriculture and the environmental damage associated with them had the effect of undermining survival economies and local 'economies of natural ecological processes'. These sorts of expansions constitute what Shiva calls 'first world bioimperialism' (1993: 78), because they are seen as involving 'the transfer of biological resources from the colonies to the centres of imperial power, and the displacement of local biodiversity in the colonies by monocultures of raw materials for European industry' (ibid.: 83).

Many argue (see later) that the colonization of survival economies continues in the present 'age of biology'. Such contemporary colonialism, they say, is associated with the life sciences and biotechnology industry and its activities in biodiversity-rich countries such as India, Brazil and Malaysia. Life sciences extend into major aspects of life – food, health, reproduction, and the environment – and biotechnology is the primary technology. Tony Blair, the current UK Prime Minister, considers biotechnology the 'next wave of the knowledge economy' and biomedical technology is seen as 'a key driver' (Rose 2005: online). Hawken *et al.* are less enchanted with biotechnology and in *Natural Capitalism: Creating the Next Industrial Revolution* (1999) they describe it as a 'market darling'.

The life science/biotechnology industry is a major factor of production in the knowledge economy. It calls into play what is called bio-prospecting. This involves the search for biological products (seeds, crops, plant medicines) and also for new healing processes. The search is largely undertaken by the 'developed' world's biotechnology knowledge industries which include transnational drug and agro-chemical companies, integrated life science corporations and their associated university-based researchers. While Brown's (2003) discussion of the history of the work of university-based US ethnobotanists suggests that early bio-prospecting was relatively unexploitative, the views of Third World activists such as Shiva suggest that even this history was not necessarily benign. Whatever the case, Krimsky (2003) illustrates convincingly that the current links in the US between university-based biological researchers and for-profit biotechnology companies are tight – indeed so tight, he talks about 'Professors Incorporated'.

The justifications for current bio-prospecting by men 'of the worldly mind' are numerous and include the assertion that access to biological diversity allows companies to develop new and better quality agricultural, food and pharmaceutical products for the market economy. Further, the moral high ground is claimed by those who argue that such products may help to address major concerns associated with hunger and health in Third World countries. It is notable that global chemical corporations for example have re-branded themselves as life science corporations in order to mount this case, in part at least, through public advertising campaigns. Monsanto is a case in point (Shiva 2000b: 11).

Ultimately, bio-prospecting means that survival economies are drawn into a 'global assemblage' (Ong and Collier 2005) that folds together scientific, entrepreneurial, economic, legal and governmental actors and institutions. Rose (2005: online) calls this a 'virtuous alliance between state, science and commerce' and Brown (2003: 101) describes it as the 'economic and legal trajectory of biological research'. Survival economies and the indigenous knowledge associated with them are seen, within this assemblage, to possess 'exploitable knowledge' (Kenway *et al.* 2004c). For instance, botanical knowledge about healing resources is possessed by indigenous people who have survived within tropic rainforests for centuries (Brown 2003). This assemblage works towards patenting and profiting from the products and processes of nature.

When the survival economy meets the knowledge economy, it is introduced to the utilitarian and privatizing logic that lies behind property rights over knowledge. More specifically, it meets the worlds associated with notions of IP, licensing, copyright, trademarks, trade secrets and patents. As we indicated in Chapter 3, IPR are a central feature of the global knowledge economy. Further, IPR are linked to national and global governance and to major issues associated with 'free trade'. Patents are central. Patents are exclusive rights granted for new inventions according to the criteria of 'novelty, non-obviousness and utility' (Krimsky 2004: 60). Where 'prior art' exists, patents should not be awarded. Drahos and Braithwaite's book *Information Feudalism: who owns the knowledge economy?* (2002) is a valuable resource on this topic. Through meticulous research, they are able to elaborate on the manner in which such intellectual property systems operate in practice and we will draw on their insights here.

The arguments offered in support of the patenting process include the claim that the high costs of research, development and commercialization must be protected through the patent process and that without it companies will neither innovate nor financially sustain innovation. However, one of the main private purposes of patent law is to gain a monopoly on any knowledge on any topic that has the potential to be commercially important. Through the use of patents it is possible to deter or prevent others from access. Patents also mean that licences and their associated fees must be gained and paid for by others in order to invent around the patent. 'The big money in licensing comes from a vast web of patents' and from having lots of 'IP levers' at the disposal of the company, thus allowing knowledge to be 'locked in' (Drahos and Braithwaite 2002: 162). Big multinational chemical, agricultural and pharmaceutical companies have been central to 'strengthening' the patent system and they also have the greatest interest in globalizing it. The patent is abstract, mobile and readily rearticulated across diverse spheres of life. The globalization of the patent system will ensure that every country in the world recognizes patent products and processes.

According to Krimsky (2004: 60), 'Patent laws and their interpretations have given rise to patents on living organisms, natural substances and the fundamental unit of heritability – the gene.' But how to patent life forms and other products of nature has been a perplexing issue in the patent world and, over time, has involved some clever legalistic footwork on the part of the biotechnology and earlier related industries (chemical, agricultural, and pharmaceutical). Eventually, 'Step by step during the course of the 20th century living systems and their parts were absorbed into the patent system' (Drahos and Braithwaite 2002: 158). This has ultimately led to the 'break down of the once clear distinction between the products of nature and the products of human ingenuity' (Brown 2003: 102) and to the adaptation of the patent system accordingly.

How can nature be seen as an invention, a discovery, an innovation? As Drahos and Braithwaite (2002: 162) indicate, 'substances that have occurred in nature but have been isolated and purified by the discoverer may be patentable'. This is to say that novel ways of processing and using such products open the way for patents. The discovery of DNA code or what they call 'mother nature's software' (ibid.: 154), and of ways to rewrite it, opens up the possibility for what seems like an 'almost endless range of products in the global markets of agriculture, food, medicines, medical therapy and chemicals' (ibid.). Such possibilities called into play new product and process 'patent targets':

> Breakthroughs in genetic engineering provided companies with four broad patent targets. There were units of life (cells, micro-organisms, plants and animals), the molecules and other elements of those units (proteins, amino acids), the instructions for the assembly of these molecules (the DNA sequences) and the methods and processes for the analysis and manipulation of the DNA instructions and molecules.
>
> (Ibid.: 155)

The patent targets rush has been accompanied by the weakening of patent utility requirements, thus accommodating those in the position to lock up a product or process, even if its use has not yet been identified. Brown (2003: 138) indicates that this has led to what some see as the 'tragedy of the anti-commons', which involves a 'patent log jam' whereby 'multiple parties can deny access to outsiders but none of the privileged owners control enough of the property to work efficiently'.

The technical complexity of chemical science and of patent law together in the knowledge economy has ratcheted up the expertise, power and expense necessary to be involved in patenting practices. Patent policies are led globally by the big patent offices of USA, Japan and Europe that are leading a process of 'harmonization' with patent policy-makers and offices in other less powerful, developing countries. In following these dominant powers, such other countries relinquish yet further power to First World countries.

Indeed, the economic and political settlements involve North/South asymmetries of power and have been of particular benefit to the USA and European Community. Further, Drahos and Braithwaite (2002: 167) predict the development of 'biogopolies' in the twenty-first century and point out that:

> Multi-nationals may now register product patents in developing countries such as India thereby giving themselves options in those markets that they previously did not have. Patents over seeds have costs implications for agricultural economies. All states will find the gossamer threads of intangible property growing ever tighter around their economies.

They further predict that the agriculture and health sectors in developing and developed countries alike will eventually end up dependent on the 'bidding or charity of biogopolies as they make strategic commercial decisions about how to use their intellectual property rights' (ibid.: 168).

In global terms, certain international governmental bodies play a critical role in the knowledge economy, 'setting principles and legal frameworks on the patenting of biological materials and life forms' (Khor 2004: online). These are, most importantly, the World Trade Organization (WTO) and, to a much lesser extent, the World International Property Organization. Here is not the place to offer a history of the activities or significant treaty milestones of these governmental bodies with regard to survival economies, indigenous knowledge or, more specifically, their biological materials and life forms. However, several points must be made. These organizations are involved in redefining intellectual property standards in global terms but are in effect universalizing the US patent system of 'patents on life' (Shiva 2000a). The WTO developed the Trade-Related Intellectual Property Rights Agreement (TRIPS). This evolved as part of the Uruguay Round of Multilateral Trade negotiations begun in 1986 and was finally signed in 1994 in Marrakech. Drahos and Braithwaite (2002: 10) point out that:

> this was the first stage in the global recognition of an investment morality that sees knowledge as a private, rather than public, good. The intellectual property standards contained in TRIPS, obligatory on all members of the WTO, would help them to enforce that morality around the world. ... TRIPS effectively globalizes the set of intellectual property principles it contains, because most states of the world are members of, or are seeking membership of, the WTO. ... The standards of TRIPS will profoundly affect the ownership of the 21st century's two great technologies – digital technology and biotechnology.

Particular Articles of TRIPS relate to living resources and biodiversity and thus also relate to the indigenous knowledges that are usually associated with survival economies. For instance, in Third World countries, farmers' access to and ability to exchange seed is seen as severely compromised by the private property and commercial regimes of TRIPS and the giant cartels and monopolies that are supported by this regime. As Shiva (2000b: 81) argues, three processes are intensifying monopoly control over seeds, 'economic concentration, patents and intellectual property rights, and genetic engineering'.

Resisting the repetition of colonial injustice

> Diversity has got to be heard; diversity amongst the world cultures. It's not just money, money, money.
>
> (Senior staff member, Communication and Information Section, UNESCO)

We have identified the dominant features of the life sciences/biotechnology global assemblage. However, this assemblage is heterogeneous and involves counter-hegemonic actors who resist the repetition of the economic, ecological and epistemological injustices of colonialism. It is these actors who, in Derrida's terms, insist on the persistence of the 'present past'; the persistence of those who are 'no longer'. They actively listen to the ghosts of the dead. A wide range of individuals, groups and social movements is involved. In broad terms, these consist, first, of civil society and people's organizations with specific foci on such things as indigenous agriculture, knowledge, heritage and rights. Second, there are those groups with wider foci but which include such matters. This broader set involves those Third World, green and public interest groups that problematize current approaches to economics and trade and the behaviour of global corporations (we will return to these in the next section). Of course, these groups do not all speak with one voice or with exactly the same sets of interests. Broadly, however, they resist repeating the damaging past and the dangerous present in the now and the 'to come'. In this sense they also listen to the ghosts of future generations.

Such counter-hegemonic groups are critical of economic/corporate globalization – its privileging of the economy over the environment, and the desires for luxuries of the affluent over the survival needs of the poor and of the planet. Knowledge for profit is juxtaposed against knowledge for sustenance, commerce against conservation (Shiva 2000a: 47). The work of these groups includes such things as raising public awareness of and knowledge about the issues, networking and building alliances, lobbying national governments and international governmental agencies and other global fora such as the various pertinent United Nations directorates. For example, they may lobby national governments for the enactment of national laws that in some way subvert TRIPS. These groups may also work in unison with individual countries (e.g. India) and groups of Third World countries (e.g. in Africa and Central and Latin America), lobbying international bodies such as the WTO to reform TRIPS. Further, they mount legal challenges to certain patents in various national patents offices. Electronic activism has become an important resource for resistance as the Third World Network (TWN) website (2005: online) ably demonstrates.

Our focus here is on the directions of the oppositional arguments that such groups are mounting with regard to 'bio-prospecting' and its effects on survival economies. A major concern amongst those who seek to resist the repetition of unjust colonial knowledge practices is what they call biopiracy. The Rural Advancement Foundation International coined this term. This became the action group on Erosion Technology and Concentration (ETC Group) in 2003, which is a member of the Coalition Against Biopiracy (COB) and is part of the global campaign against biopiracy. COB is an informal collection of activist organizations that formed in 1995 in Jakarta in response to the Convention on Biological Diversity. This Coalition keenly monitors and resists biopiracy around the world. The ETC Group (2005: online) defines biopiracy thus:

> Biopiracy refers to the appropriation of the knowledge and genetic resources of farming and indigenous communities by individuals or institutions seeking exclusive monopoly control (usually patents or plant breeders' rights) over these resources and knowledge.

As numerous clearing houses and websites devoted to the matter indicate, concerns related to biopiracy include: the 'unauthorized use' or 'theft' of indigenous resources (e.g. plants, animals, organs, micro-organisms, genes) and knowledge about the use of such resources; the lack of proper acknowledgement; the inequitable sharing of benefits; the failure to comply with the spirit of patent criteria (novelty, non-obviousness and usefulness); and the translation of indigenous biological knowledge and common wealth into a source of revenue for wealthy people, nations, and corporations.

Broadly, the argument is that the genetic and other materials pirated and patented by certain fields of biotechnology were originally, and over considerable periods of time, identified, developed and put to use by indigenous peoples in their day-to-day lives. Well-known examples include basmati rice, pepper, ginger, mustard and neem (Shiva 2000b: 81) Through the patenting process, 'the companies claim the exclusive right to produce and sell many "modified" plants and animals, which have been manipulated to contain selected foreign genes' says Martin Khor (2005: online), Director of the Third World Network. For example, in an article called 'The US Patent System Legalizes Theft and Biopiracy', Shiva (1999: online) argues that:

> Biopiracy and patenting of indigenous knowledge is a double theft because, firstly, it allows theft of creativity and innovation, and secondly, the exclusive rights established by patents on stolen knowledge, steal economic options of everyday survival on the basis of our indigenous

> biodiversity and indigenous knowledge. Over time, the patents can be used to create monopolies and make everyday products highly priced.

The irony here is that the biodiversity of the Third World is treated by the First World as freely available, but once slightly modified and patented, treats it as its own private property. Further perverse reversals include the fact that the protection of local knowledges can be defined as a barrier to free trade. While more broadly, trade and commerce have triumphed over notions of the intellectual and biological commons to such an extent that sharing knowledge can be defined by biotechnology companies as IP theft – as biopiracy.

Biotechnology companies are seen to claim the greatest benefits here, although the extent of such benefits is much debated. However, it is widely acknowledged that the global pharmaceutical industry reaps startling levels of profit with blockbuster drugs 'yielding profit margins approaching 30% ... three times higher than that of the American corporate sector as a whole' (Brown 2003: 103). The outcomes for indigenous peoples are that they either get inadequate financial compensation or none at all. Further, they may then have to buy back in some form or another the knowledge that is their own. They may be unable to afford the buy-back and, as a consequence, may be excluded from their own knowledge and even criminalized if they use such knowledge without permission – becoming 'trespassers in their own cultures' (Drahos and Braithwaite 2002: 201).

The Coalition Against Biopiracy clearly understands the ever-present possibility that haunting might fade, allowing forgetting to transpire. It has thus sponsored the high-profile and provocative Captain Hook Awards since 1995. Whereas the knowledge economy continues to thrive on the basis of creative destruction, the Captain Hook Awards engage in a form of creative deconstruction. Directly thumbing its nose at major international treaties, the CAB has held each of its award ceremonies at the Convention on Biological Diversity (CBD) meetings in Nairobi (2000), The Hague (2002) and Kuala Lumpur (2004). Recognizing the pull and power of web activism, it publicizes these events on the Captain Hook Awards website (2005: online). Featuring visuals of skull and cross-bones, pirates and pirate ships, it called for nominations for the *Outstanding Achievements in Biopiracy* 2004 Awards, asking:

> What's the most outrageous biopiracy case in your country? Who's ripping off indigenous knowledge in your community? Who's monopolizing your genes or patenting your plants? Has anyone trademarked your favorite patron saint? We need your help to identify the Greediest, Most Offensive and Dangerous biopirates from across the globe.
>
> (Ibid.)

It offers Captain Hook Awards in different categories including, Worst National Behaviour, Worst International Convention, Greediest, Most

Offensive, Most Dangerous. But it also makes what it calls Cog Awards ('so-named because cogs were ships designed to repel pirate attacks'), inviting nominations for 'those institutions, peoples' organizations, and governments that have fended off acts of biopiracy, defeated predatory patents, or defended the intellectual and cultural integrity of farmers and indigenous peoples'. The categories here include Best Individual Advocate, Best Peoples' Defense, Best Legal Defense, Best National Defense, Most Imaginative.

Linking politics and parody[3] and spoofing such awards as the Academy Awards in a News Release about the 2004 awards ceremony in Kuala Lumpur, it calls its awards 'uncoveted', explains that they are 'for infamous and outstanding malachievements', talks of its 'Hall of Shame', and of the possibility of a 'Lifetime Achievement Award' for Monsanto. The website begins:

> *Ahoy and Welcome to The 2004 Captain Hook Awards*
> It has been more than a decade since the CBD entered into force, but biopiracy is flourishing and the notion of 'benefit-sharing' is merely a charade that even helps to legitimate it. In 2004, it's still smooth sailing and easy looting for biopirates who use intellectual property to plunder genetic resources and pillage traditional knowledge.
>
> (Ibid.)

The COB's many Captain Hook awards draw to public attention the perverse IP reversals noted above. For instance, its Worst International Convention award went to the World Intellectual Property Organization (WIPO) with the following explanation:

> WIPO takes the prize for 'Worst International Convention' for two initiatives. First, for proposing a new global patent system under the 'Substantive Patent Law Treaty', which would override national patent laws and development strategies, in order to pave the way for a 'world patent' granted directly by WIPO, facilitating one-stop shopping for exclusive monopolies. And for promoting the idea that traditional knowledge can be 'protected' in the context of intellectual property. WIPO has been promoting intellectual property as a solution to protecting indigenous peoples and their heritage, of which traditional knowledge is an indivisible part. WIPO has failed to acknowledge that intellectual property rights are incompatible with the protection of traditional knowledge, being the source of the problem, not the solution.
>
> (Ibid.)

The Cog Awards are allocated to those who actively resist institutionalized IP arrangements and who thus illustrate activist possibilities. For instance the award for the Best Legal Defense in 2004 was awarded to Greenpeace International, Misereor, the Mexican government, and other concerned parties.

> It challenged, in May 2001, Dupont's patent on all maize varieties with higher oil and oleic acid content – including traditional maize varieties. Granted by the European Patent Office in August 2000, EP 0744888 B1 covered 'Corn grains and products with improved oil composition', the result of plant breeding done at Iowa State University and the University of Illinois (USA). After a challenge made by Greenpeace and Misereor, and letters from the Mexican Government, the European Patent Office reviewed the opposition in February 2003 and announced the revocation of the patent on February 12, 2003.
>
> (Ibid.)

Views vary about how best to resist biopiracy and clearly not all counter hegemonic actions involve political parody and public shaming practices. These are an anathema to the hyperrationality of the knowledge economy. From the point of view of the knowledge economy's dominant institutions such political practices are seen as more irritating than illuminating.

There are also divergent views about how, in the current context, indigenous people can best benefit from their biological resources and knowledge. Numerous international conventions speak to this issue (see further Hawken *et al.* 1999: 322). For example, even though it has been overshadowed by TRIPS and the WTO and is mercilessly criticized by the ETC group (2004), the United Nations *Convention on Biological Diversity* (CBD) signed at the Earth Summit at Rio de Janeiro in 1992 remains a significant document. It seeks to acknowledge national sovereignty over biological resources. One outcome of a focus on the violation of indigenous IPR has been on the possibilities of formalized partnerships, benefit sharing, negotiation and amelioration. For instance, one claim here is that bilateral contracts between source countries and biotechnology companies which elaborate the rules of benefit sharing, have the potential to result in benefits for local people as well as the other parties to the contract. In discussing specific examples of such arrangements, Brown (2003: 140) explains that:

> Governments and local communities now routinely set stringent conditions on bio-prospecting projects. Foreign scientists must commit themselves to close collaboration with local counterparts, provide host-country institutions with equipment and training, and agree to profit sharing arrangements. Indigenous leaders may demand that visiting scholars pay for access to local expertise and perhaps provide communities with badly needed health clinic and school buildings.

However, there are several reasons why benefit sharing and partnerships of the sort parodied and critiqued by the Captain Hook Awards can be and indeed have proved problematic – even when they claim to be in the interests of indigenous people themselves. While possibly attractive in broad principle, the distribution of benefits can be very difficult when confronted with the political and bureaucratic complexities of practice, a matter well demonstrated in Brown's careful analysis of various examples of bio-prospecting. From the point of view of biotechnology companies, the complications include the fact that it is hard to calculate what would be considered a fair trade and realistic remuneration, particularly given that the 'samples' or knowledge collected may not necessarily lead to a profitable new product. Indeed, Brown (2003: 273) draws on a range of case study sources to argue that, since the COB in 1992, no economic profit has been generated from the conversion of indigenous knowledge into commercial pharmaceutical products. Further, if the relevant sample or knowledge can be found in several places within and across nations, it is not always clear who the benefits are to be negotiated and shared with. The political complexities and ethical ambiguities involved have meant delays and frustrations for those who have attempted to share benefits.

However, from the perspective of traditional owners of the plants, animals, human genes and knowledge, such problems are differently and more deeply manifest. Indeed, what is to be understood as the 'best interests' of indigenous people in these circumstances is not always clear. They may be unaware of the potential commercial value of their knowledge and thus not well positioned to ensure fair benefit sharing. But even if they are aware, establishing value is complicated and made more so by the matter of establishing ownership in the first place. When different groups in different locations believe they own the species or the knowledge, this makes it difficult to establish a claim, may lead to unhelpful competition and may ultimately reduce the benefits to all parties. A further difficulty arises around the matter of who is entitled to speak for whom: 'Can the state speak for them or must they be allowed to speak for themselves?' (ibid.: 112). When indigenous groups are at odds with the national government of the country within which they live, difficulties can arise with regard to who best represents them, who negotiates benefit sharing arrangements and on what basis.

In some instances, the notion of ownership itself may be the problem. As an entry in the Wikipedia Free Encyclopaedia, an open-source encyclopaedia, explains, some do not support the idea 'that it is a natural right to own plants, animals and human genes'. The entry goes on to state:

> Resources belong to the community, private property has no meaning. They argue that what is 'wrong' is not so much the appropriation of somebody else's property, but rather to consider private, natural resources that should stay public.
>
> (2005: online)

While it is certainly the case that the indigenous knowledges of survival economies have become caught up in the knowledge economy's worlds of property and patents, such knowledges do not necessarily readily match the requirements of IP systems. The notion of public knowledge is an anathema to IPR systems, as, indeed, is any indigenous knowledge that sees biodiversity as a commons and the generation of livelihoods as in partnership with diverse species (Shiva 2000a: 134).

Some life sciences/biotechnology resistance activists are very much opposed to joining the current IP patent game. The TRIPS agenda is increasingly seen to have elevated trade and IP rules above environmental treaties and national laws. Further, colonial history and contemporary North/South asymmetrical power politics have led them to see benefit sharing schemes as pseudo and tokenistic and ultimately on the terms of biotechnology colonizing bodies. Shiva argues (1999: online) that:

> A globalised IPR regime which denies the knowledge and innovations of the Third World, which allows such innovations to be treated as inventions in the US, which legalises monopolistic exclusive rights by granting of patents based on everyday, common-place indigenous knowledge, is a regime which needs to be overhauled and amended.

Shiva believes that there is a need for common property knowledge systems that will 'recognize the indigenous utilization of biodiversity and collective, cumulative innovation embodied in indigenous knowledge systems' and 'preserve the integrity of the indigenous knowledge systems on which our everyday survival is based' (ibid.). These, she says, should reflect the 'triple plurality' of intellectual modes, of property systems and of systems of combinations (Shiva 2000a: 35).

Those who take a stand against TRIPS and the globalization of the patent system usually seek to modify the TRIPS regime while at the same time developing alternatives to it. They have, for instance, tried to 'humanise intellectual property' by pushing for a 'development agenda' in the World International Property Organization (Khor 2005: online). They may push for the extensive national documentation and registration of indigenous knowledges and the development of diverse, less convoluted and expensive IPR systems. They may argue for TRIPS to be subordinate to the CBD or other international statements such as United Nations 1997 *Protection of the Heritage of Indigenous People*, commonly known as the Daes Report. Further, given that many Third World countries view life forms – genetic, animal, plant – as common heritage and exclude them from the patent system, they may promote the establishment of the principle of *sui generis*, to allow national constitutions' 'self standing' laws to protect the innovations of indigenous and farming communities. Alternatively, they may seek the total exclusion of patents on life forms.

Other partnership benefit-sharing issues arise, at least in part, because the indigenous knowledge of survival economies is not readily integrated into modern scientific practices. Indigenous knowledge is often tacit knowledge and as such is not readily codified and communicated beyond the local people. As nature and culture are often entangled, the knowledge may not necessarily be replicable when stripped of its context. Further, indigenous science and technology systems and those of modern science with its formal and highly bureaucratized validation processes, are difficult to reconcile. They are in many ways incompatible and incommensurate, each regarding the other as 'other'. 'A clash of paradigms, worldviews and cultures is involved; in short, fundamentally different approaches to human and environmental survival are apparent' (Shiva 2000a: 28). The survival economy either implicitly or explicitly challenges many of the *dominant* premises of modern Western science systems. Shiva's work comprehensively illustrates this argument.

Her challenge is mounted, in the first instance, around her critique of what she calls 'monocultures of the mind' (1993). Such monocultures involve unidimensional and uni-directional sensibilities that see problems in isolation from each other rather than in their interdependency, and lock out or marginalize alternatives. They lead to the assumption that dominant ways of knowing and being are the best or only way and to a view that these should be imposed on others – substituting control for self-organization. Monocultural sensibilities involve 'reductionist knowledge, mechanistic technologies and the commodification of resources' (Shiva 2000a: 8). They have led to the global pre-eminence of the industrialization of fisheries, forestry, medicine and farming and to the dominance of the market economy over survival/natures economies. For instance, 'global market integration converts millions of acres of forests and farms into industrial monocultures displacing and destroying both biodiversity and the cultural diversity of local communities' (ibid.: 15–16).

Shiva illustrates such claims with many examples, including the monocultivation and monocultures associated with scientific industrial forestry and the introduction of pine and eucalyptus plantations. These treat natural forests only as a source of industrial and commercial timber and refuse the 'multiple functions of the forest as a source of food and agriculture and a multidimensional knowledge system for forest dwellers and forest users' (Shiva 1993: 18). Further, the monocultures and global trade associated with industrial agriculture have led to the global dominance of only four species – rice, maize, wheat, and soybean. In terms of the world's food consumption, a total of 34 varieties of grain have taken the place of crop diversity involving at least 7,000 species that were cultivated and provided food over considerable periods of time (Shiva 2000b). Farming around the world has altered as a consequence of industrial agriculture and associated patent regimes – the so-called 'Green Revolution'. Less and less does farming produce nutritious and diverse foodstuffs and more and more is farming absorbed into markets for genetically-engineered and corporately-patented agricultural seeds, herbicides, pesticides, and irrigation systems. Farming has become dependent on chemicals.

Monocultures also deny economic alternatives outside the market and destroy the economic viability of the world's poorest people. Shiva (2000a: 131) explains that:

> When monocultures of export crops replace food crops, local people go hungry. When herbicides wipe out biodiversity, the poor . . . are deprived of food, cattle fodder and medicine. Whenever we engage in consumption or production patterns that take more than we need, we are engaging in a violent economic order.

Overall, Shiva (1993) argues that the diversion of increasingly scarce resources (forests, water and land) involves the highly inequitable distribution of the costs of the economic growth from the over-developed First World to the Third World, which pays for the prosperity of the privileged. This contributes to global instability and insecurity.

Monocultures of the mind and of 'the ground' – or material things (ibid.) – obstruct perceptions of the multiple benefits and uses of biodiversity. Indeed, they screen from view alternative knowledge and technology systems, as Shiva (1993) explains in detail. Further, they *reduce* understandings of biodiversity to 'single functions of single species' and promote patterns of utilization and consumption that not only wipe out biodiversity broadly defined, but put monocultures and indeed monopolies in its place, with highly destructive consequences (2000a: 103). Shiva (1993: 50) maintains:

> A crucial characteristic of monocultures is that they do not merely displace alternatives; they destroy their own basis. They are neither tolerant of other systems, nor are they able to reproduce themselves sustainably.

The sustainability of forest resources demonstrates this. Diversity and sustainability are ecologically linked because 'diversity offers the multiplicity of interactions, which can heal ecological disturbance to any part of the system' (ibid.: 77). The biological productivity of the forest is rooted in its ecological diversity. Scientific industrial forestry degrades the forest, destroying the ecological conditions that enable it to renew itself and contribute to water storage and flood management. It is therefore 'not only destructive but also not sustainable' (ibid.: 50). Ultimately, Shiva argues, this sort of practice is leading the planet towards biological and social unsustainability.

The 'to come' – surviving the knowledge economy?

> The information society is one step towards an honest society and an honest society is one step towards a wisdom society.
>
> (Senior staff member, Communication and Information Section, UNESCO)

As we said at the outset of this chapter, the condition of any presence is living-on. This involves taking responsibility for 'legacies beyond the living present', Derrida (1994: 187) says. Such sentiments apply as much to economies as to ecology. So what of the 'to come'?

The emergence and increasing dominance of the life sciences, biotechnology and TRIPS has been accompanied by serious worldwide scientific concerns about biodiversity and sustainable growth, climate change, pollution, resource depletion, bio-hazards, bio-safety, poverty and inequality. Indeed, many such ethical, environmental and socio-economic issues have been disregarded by TRIPS. The notion of public interest science is relevant here. What this means is developed at length by Krimsky (2003). In short, it accepts the obligation to fearlessly question the status quo and to put science to use in the interests of better, more sustainable, societies. Lowe (2005: 18) calls this 'sustainability science'. One example is the Australian Commonwealth Science and Research Organisation's (CSIRO) *Sustainable Ecosystems* programme, which is 'focused on maintaining the sustainability of Australia's landscapes, environments and communities' (2005: online). Such concerns in the scientific world have been increasingly accompanied by widespread popular anxiety which has extended beyond that associated with indigenous knowledge activism. This is expressed through tens of thousands of institutions and organizations around the world, ranging from land trusts to outdoor clubs, from church groups to charitable foundations. Hawken *et al.* (1999: 315) observe that 'collectively these have become the world's largest and fastest growing activist movement' which, through its various 'mandates, directives, principles, declarations and other statements of purpose', shares a broad consensus to defend human life and the life of the planet and work towards a sustainable world. They recognize that:

> The *natural capital* on which civilization depends to create economic prosperity, is rapidly declining. ... As more people and businesses place greater strain on living systems, limits to prosperity are coming to be determined by natural capital rather than industrial prowess.
>
> (Ibid.: 2, original emphasis)

The research on this matter is voluminous and points to some considerable apprehension for 'the ghosts of those who are not yet born' (Derrida 1994: xix).

In the context of this parallel set of concerns, survival economies are seen to provide further 'exploitable knowledge'. However, in this instance, the knowledge is about biodiversity and sustainability. Survival economies are seen to have the potential to provide possible solutions to the overdeveloped world's environmental problems. Their knowledge about 'the economy of natural ecological processes' and their 'indigenous science and technology systems' is in demand. And there are now numerous attempts to integrate such knowledge, of say botany and breeding, into modern scientific environmental and land care practices. For instance, Brown (2003: 205–6) tells of the ways in which indigenous knowledge has been incorporated into environmental planning and land management of endangered arctic and subarctic ecosystems, using the example of the local Inuit's knowledge of the

Hudson Bay eider population. The Inuit's knowledge exceeded that of environmental planners and, when drawn on, enabled the planners to better protect the eider population across the Arctic region as a whole.

Shiva asks 'How can we, as members of the earth community, reinvent security to ensure the survival of all species, and the survival and future of diverse cultures?' (2004: 64). Arguing that natural and cultural diversity are the main sources of wealth, Shiva calls for 'diverse ways of thinking and living' (1993: 7). She argues for the recognition of multiple knowledge systems as well as for modern ecological and context-dependent sustainability-oriented approaches to the life sciences. Knowledge for survival, she says, 'is based on ecology – it is evolved collectively and is freely shared to improve the well-being of all life, including human life, not the displacement of other ways of knowing, other objectives for knowledge creation and other modes of knowledge sharing' (2000a: 35).

Biodiversity (genetic, species and ecosystem) and cultural diversity go hand in hand. Diverse ecosystems give rise to diverse life forms and to diverse cultures. And, the evolving co-dependence of cultures, life forms and habitats has conserved the planet's biological diversity (Shiva 1993). For instance, 'ecological knowledge of biodiversity has given rise to cultural rules for conservation reflected in notions of sacredness and taboos' (ibid.: 65) but, according to Shiva, this is only part of the story. Biodiversity must also be seen as embodying 'multiple species in multiple interactions performing multiple functions' (Shiva 2000a: 103). The future of the planet is understood as closely connected to the future of biological and cultural diversity. Survival economies exemplify these key points.

The wide range of survival and sustenance livelihoods in the Third World – hunting and gathering, pastoral, peasant and fishing – has arisen in relation to the variety of ecosystems in the most biodiversity-rich parts of the world. Involving diverse species, cultures and knowledge systems, their survival depends on their intricate knowledge of biodiversity and their skilful and sustainable use of its wealth. Shiva calls this 'the wealth of the poor' and explains that biodiversity is put to use for nutrition, health care, shelter, energy, crafts and ceremony. Ecological and economic securities are tightly intertwined. Extraction and exploitation of nature as raw material and a source of profit is not the dominant paradigm here. Rather, as we suggested earlier, the paradigm is ecological and is premised on notions of complexity, respect, reciprocity and responsibility – it involves restorative justice. All living organisms are viewed as 'complex, self organised and constantly changing dynamic systems' linked to each other in 'webs of reciprocal life support' (Shiva 2000b: 27). As we have said, Shiva calls this 'nature's economy' and argues that it is the foundation of all other economies:

> Those who depend on biodiversity for survival know that they must keep that diversity alive. They understand the importance of maintaining the integrity of nature's processes, cycles and rhythms.
>
> (2000a: 124)

Survival economies' economic values therefore merge with their ecological values, which acknowledge 'the intrinsic value of each species' (ibid.: 29). They are to be conserved as well as utilized for current and future human needs and livelihoods. For instance, biodiversity based on organic agriculture first meets the needs of its ecological and social base – 'the earth, other species, and local households and communities'. It then trades its 'genuine surpluses' (ibid.: 122). This involves meeting the varying needs of ecosystems and diverse peoples. It also speaks to principles of ethics and justice. In these ways, then, survival economies express a deep understanding of the ways in which one's actions in the present have consequences for the future, and accept responsibility for past, present and future.

What does sustainability science look like on the ground? How does it integrate diverse knowledges and share benefits? How is a closer integration of ecology and economics effected? Is there a sting in the tail/tale of sustainability science? A recent example of a benefit-sharing, partnership approach is Desert Knowledge Australia (2005: online).[4] Taking up a major imperative of knowledge economy policy it combines university-based researchers, governments and private sponsors, and recognizes the benefits of sharing ideas for the production of knowledge and wealth. It brings together the extensive scientific and technical knowledge of the knowledge economy in Australia, 'as well as thousands of years of accumulated indigenous expertise and other skills relevant to desert livelihoods'. It stresses 'harmony' between 'western style and indigenous communities'; the 'sustainability' of 'the local and global environment' and 'wealth creation'. It describes the latter as 'Developing viable business and employment opportunities capable of supporting an internationally competitive lifestyle for the people of the desert.' Desert Knowledge Australia is building national and international networks and partnerships to 'undertake the research, product development and marketing needed for thriving desert knowledge economies . . . to create an economically and socially sustainable future'. One aspect of such work is 'Intellectual Property arrangements for communities to progress commercial opportunities' (ibid.). It points out that 'One third of the world's land surface is desert' and that 'one sixth of the world's population' lives in such semi-arid and arid lands'. It argues that Australian desert knowledge has great commercial potential in other desert countries.

Clearly, in this example, competition, commercialization and the market are the dominant motifs. Knowledge is not to be 'freely shared to improve the well-being of all life' in other arid locales as Shiva might suggest. The connotations of 'harmony' and 'sustainability' are, it seems, to be restricted accordingly. All the problems we identified earlier regarding benefit sharing remain. Further, questions might well be asked about the extent to which indigenous Australians in the desert want an 'internationally competitive lifestyle'. Whether the sacred knowledges of indigenous people and the cultural practices associated with their desert knowledge can actually be harmonized with Western practices remains a moot point. Further, indigenous cultural connections with the land, their sense of ownership of it, suggest that commodifying the land runs counter to this deep history.

Another on-the-ground example of sustainability science is the CSIRO's *Sustainable Ecosystems* programme's project *Australian Native Foods*. This involves the CSIRO working with Aboriginal communities and Australian industry. It is 'seeking ways to lower production costs and increase product quality in order to meet the growing demand for a variety of food ingredients from Australian native plants, seeds and fruits' (2005: online), it also taps into a niche market. The project's benefits are seen to be that it:

- conserves wild resources and helps protect biodiversity;
- utilizes Aboriginal knowledge and values traditional lore;
- contributes to combating salinity problems by introducing more perennials;
- encourages farmers to diversify from traditional crops; and
- creates incomes and jobs for Aboriginal and rural communities (ibid.).

What is called 'wild harvesting' and growing demand for such foods are seen to place too much pressure on supply, running the risk that some species might become unsustainable. Hence, says the CSIRO, it is 'researching techniques for sustainable native food cultivation'. The CSIRO scientist Dr Maarten Ryder (2005: online), is quoted on the website as saying:

> We hope the native food project will encourage producers to grow native foods commercially ... What we're doing is working with Aboriginal knowledge about these amazing foods from the Australian environment and putting that together with western farming methods and cultivation methods.

Morse, who is also working on a 'bush tucker' project, says that while Australia's bush-tucker industry has strong potential, it needs 'focussing': 'There are a lot of potential crops from central Australia – bush tomatoes and raisins, desert yams ... even truffles. But to overcome the vagaries of the seasons, we need to start establishing plantations close to the Aboriginal communities where they can be better managed.'

It seems that nature's economy ('the vagaries of the seasons') and indigenous knowledge are to make way for 'western farming methods' including plantations, for monocultures of cultivation. While the project recognizes multiple knowledge systems, one can infer that Aboriginal knowledge is seen in a service role, and that so-called western methods of farming are deemed preferable. The extent to which sustainability *and* diversity are able to work hand in hand here remains an open question. If, as Shiva argues, biodiversity requires multiplicity with regard to species, interactions, and functions, then plantations of bush food suggest that biodiversity itself is at stake here.

In both these examples of sustainability science at least, sustainably surviving the knowledge economy means ultimately subscribing to the market and to modified monocultures. This suggests that those involved have only partially reconciled with the spirits of the past and the future.

* * *

We have shown that survival economies haunt the knowledge economy in several ways. The 'living subjectivity' of survival economies includes imprints of past colonial and ecological subjugation. They have been exploited by earlier market economies and their 'living-on' involves traces of the people and species whose ways of life have previously been exploited or destroyed by men 'of the worldly mind'. This 'living on' also invokes the ever-present possibility of the repetition in the present and the future of past practices of subjugation. This depleting past and dangerous present have led advocates for survival economies to resist repetition, to invoke the ghosts of colonialism and to do so in the name of justice. In many senses they are following Derrida, who says:

> If I am getting ready to speak at length about ghosts, inheritance, and generations, generations of ghosts, which is to say about certain *others* who are not present, nor presently living, either to us, or outside us, it is in the name of *justice*.
>
> (1994: xix, original emphases)

Those indigenous knowledge activists, who conjure the ghosts of this past, recognize that the life sciences/biotechnology industries are repeating such subjugation in the present in the form of bioprospecting, the increasing globalization of intellectual property (specifically patent) systems and monocultural approaches to knowledge and production. Survival economies have their own 'natural capital'; their own indigenous knowledge about nature's abundance. This, we established, makes them valuable to the knowledge economy and vulnerable to its view of knowledge and relationships as 'uncontaminated presence'. The knowledge economy has little respect for those who are no longer or who are not yet there, to paraphrase Derrida. Accusations of biopiracy are one means whereby activists try to encourage the knowledge economy to 'reckon with' spirits, as Derrida suggests. But, we have indicated that such an encouragement to converse with ghosts happens on many political, legal and symbolic fronts in the global state, science, and commerce assemblage. It involves multiple forms of amelioration with varying levels of acceptability.

Survival economies have science and technology systems and views of ownership that set them apart from the market economy and its more recent incarnation, the knowledge economy. Throughout this chapter we have made the argument that natural and cultural diversity and common ownership are the subordinated differences that arise to haunt the knowledge economy. These differences are the conditions of possibility for changing the present relationship between economics and ecology. When indigenous knowledge activists mobilize these differences, when they invoke the 'spectral moment', they issue invitations to responsibility and justice for the now and the 'to come'. Many people around the world who share a concern about sustainability have accepted these ghostly invitations. They recognize that survival economies possess knowledge with the potential to contribute to planetary survival. As we have shown, some sustainability scientists have accepted such invitations with reservations, defaulting to a monocultural market logic. But as Derrida reminds us ghosts don't die, they always remain and return. It is thus probable that such hesitations will prompt further spectral exchanges.

Notes

1 Many theorists of development associated with the World Bank subscribe to such views (Stiglitz 2002). Herman Daly, who has been a senior advisor to the World Bank, is an exception here. He has long argued for a close integration of economics and ecology – for ecologically sustainable economies, the fair distribution of resources intergenerationally and economic attention to the needs of all species (e.g. 1994, 1997, 1998).

2 The niceties of the differences between these concepts are not of concern here but for a discussion see Wenzel (1999).

3 See Robb and Bullen (2004) for our attempt to satirize the knowledge economy.

4 The Desert Knowledge Cooperative Research Centre, a companion to Desert Knowledge Australia, is 'a national research network linking indigenous and local knowledge with science and education to improve desert livelihoods'. It seeks, amongst much, to build 'sustainable livelihoods for desert people' in part through what it calls 'place based products' such as 'living Aboriginal culture and wide open spaces' and 'bush products', also called 'natural plant resources'.

Foreboding?

> From the foldings of its robe, it brought two children; wretched, abject, frightful, hideous, miserable.
> "Spirit! Are they yours?" Scrooge could say no more.
> "They are Man's," said the Spirit, looking down upon them.
> "And they cling to me ... This boy is Ignorance. This girl is Want. Beware them both ... but most of all this boy, for on his brow I see that written which is Doom."
>
> (Dickens, *A Christmas Carol*, [1843] 2003: 92–4)

The Ghost of Christmas Present shows Scrooge the 'ignorance' and 'want' that both industrial capitalism and he, as its ideal subject, deny. The ghost cautions each that if they continue to deny these things they will ultimately make them worse. It warns them to pay particular attention to ignorance, as choosing to remain unaware will result in certain doom.

At the outset we explained that Derrida wants us all to believe in ghosts. He suggests that when ghosts return to haunt the living we must resist the urge to conjure them away, although they may be disturbing, and attempt to fully converse with them instead. He argues further that:

> The 'scholar' of the future, the 'Intellectual' of tomorrow ... should learn to live by learning not how to make conversation with the ghost but how to talk with him, with her, how to let them speak or how to give them back speech ... they are always *there*, specters, even if they do not exist, even if they are no longer, even if they are not yet. They give us to rethink the 'there' as soon as we open our mouths.
>
> (Derrida 1994: 176, original emphasis)

According to Derrida, as we indicated right at the start, it is only by speaking to, and of ghosts, by engaging in discourse with and on them, that we can acknowledge the responsibilities that lie beyond the present moment. And, as 'scholars of the future' in the now, we accepted his provocative argument about the virtues of conversing with ghosts, and adopted his hauntology methodology.

We identified the spectral economies that the knowledge economy ignorantly belittles or ignores – the risk, gift, libidinal and survival economies. Our central premise throughout has been that these alternative economies can be understood as ghosts that haunt and disturb the knowledge economy by questioning its current economic course, challenging its narrow and reductionist logic and confronting its underlying assumptions. These ghosts caution the knowledge economy against the impeding doom that may result if it continues to measure the value of knowledge mainly in monetary terms, and if it remains arrogant about, or wilfully ignorant of, other economies with different social, cultural, ecological, and ethical values.

Spectral risk, gift, libidinal and survival economies are the silences around which knowledge economy discourse is ordered. In this book, these silences have been interpreted and incarnated as haunting spectres. The ghosts have been given a position from which to speak, and an opportunity to be heard, and we have shown how our obligations as scholars to the past, present and the future are dependent on listening to what they have to say. We have brought the knowledge economy into 'conversation' with its ghosts: those spectral economies whose haunting presence it ignores. Having given them back speech, to paraphrase Derrida, what, in sum, have we learnt?

The knowledge economy is an economy of perverse paradoxes: it tries to deny that ghosts exist, but at the same time seeks to banish them. It does not believe in its own ghosts, let alone the ghosts of other economies. It preserves the purity of its presence by conjuring away its own ambiguous history. Instead, it claims to be definitive, to be the first and last word on knowledge and economics. But its ghosts have different stories to tell, as we explained in Chapter 1. These stories contain the many meanings of the knowledge economy itself as these have altered over time, over place, across disciplines, and as they have shifted to and fro between the world of scholarship and the world of policy. These stories also draw attention to the ways in which the notion of 'economy' has become collapsed with the notion of 'society', imagining fruitlessly that the problems of society can be resolved through economics alone. The ghosts of the knowledge economy itself point to the limitations of this conceit and the shaky foundations upon which its hegemonic status is built.

The spectre of the risk economy haunts the knowledge economy with the unforeseeable future that it seeks to know and control. However, in its undecidability the ghost casts this illusion of certitude into doubt. In Chapter 2, we showed that the ghost of the risk economy raises the possibility that the formula for economic growth in the knowledge economy may endanger future generations. In the knowledge economy, risk as a calculation of probability pretends to know the future, this actually conceals uncertainty. The knowledge economy suffers from the delusion of exclusion. It claims to know what can't be known. In effect, it excludes the unknowable – the arcane. Its only responsibility, it seems, is to take no risks with risk. In contrast, the risk economy is premised on the certainty of uncertainty.

However, this does not absolve us of the responsibilities to make decisions about the future, and these decisions must bear an ethico-political weight.

The spectre of the gift economy haunts the knowledge economy with the shadows of knowledge from the past that it seeks to leave behind. However, it is not so easy to exorcise the ghost, to conjure it away. In Chapter 3, we showed that the so-called 'archaic' gift economy has been resurrected as a counter to the knowledge economy. The dead have been brought back for a reason, to remind us of three central obligations that the knowledge economy conveniently denies: to give, to receive and to repay. The knowledge economy is a grasping economy, its only obligation is to acquire without constraint and reciprocity, and, therefore, it ignores the gift-like qualities of knowledge. Knowledge is not a gift given freely, it is buoyant with powerful obligations, and we indicated that these honorific obligations are the enduring obligations of any generative and generous economy.

The spectre of the libidinal economy haunts the knowledge economy to make it recognize the full extent of the artistic imagination – its expansive complexity. In Chapter 4, we showed how, within the libidinal economy, the libidinal energies of the arts cannot be readily constrained by the knowledge economy. The knowledge economy either denies the merits of the artistic imagination, seeing it as merely cultural, or it seeks to harness the artistic imagination and views it as merely commercial. Either way it diminishes and marginalizes the civilizing and critical purpose of the arts. The knowledge economy is a reductive economy that both commodifies and colonizes the imagination. However, we indicated that the imagination cannot be governed by government, or limited by logic, it is by its very nature excessive, and the leaky libidinal 'intensities' of the arts cannot be contained.

The spectre of the survival economy haunts the knowledge economy with the 'living-on' of those who are already dead and the 'to come' of the not yet born. It speaks against the knowledge economy's tendency to repeat the injustices of the past in the present, and its failure to attend in the here and now to the needs of the yet to be. The knowledge economy has a highly restricted view of the nature of knowledge. It is a dogmatic and destructive economy: plundering the abundance of the poor in the interests of avarice. In Chapter 5, we showed that central to the survival economy are natural and cultural diversity. It is a replenishing economy that is steeped in the knowledge of nature, and, as such, it holds the conditions of possibility to sustain the planet.

Collectively these chapters indicate that the ghosts of alternative economies arise to draw attention to the inherent instability of the knowledge economy, to contest the certainty of its economic dogma by offering alternative perspectives. Laclau (1995: 86) comments on the politics of Derrida's theory of haunting, stating:

> Without the constitutive dislocation that inhabits all hauntology – and that ontology tries to conceal – there would be no politics, just a programmed, predetermined reduction of the other to the same.

By adopting the methodology of hauntology, we have challenged the reductionist and 'no politics' proclamations of the knowledge economy. The spectres of alternative economies are indeed 'the other' of the knowledge economy. They stand apart in their difference and bring out of the shadows the knowledge and the economies that it has chosen to exclude. Risk, libidinal, gift and survival economies are spectres that reveal a far more ambivalent reality than the one admitted to by the knowledge economy. They cannot, we have suggested, be reduced to 'the same'.

It is clear from what we have said about each spectral economy that Derrida's notion of hauntology positions the ghosts of alternative economies as 'areas of undecidability' that escape from the knowledge economy's logic of non-contradiction. For Derrida, 'it is not a question of choosing between two imperatives but of inventing a way of negotiating the tension between them' (Naas 2003: 161). In this sense, and in summary, the spectral risk, gift, libidinal and survival economies exist on the threshold between two contradictory states of being: there are equal measures of certainty and uncertainty in the risk economy; what belongs in the gift economy is given and yet stays within that economy; in the libidinal economy 'intensities' are denied but they are also exploited; and in the survival economy living on depends on the living past.

By speaking to and of ghosts we have challenged the knowledge economy's programmed and predetermined path, and opened it up to other possible courses of action; we have exposed it to issues of responsibility, justice and ethics. Implicit in this strategy is the hope that the knowledge economy will not shut itself off from these ghosts, but will instead be hospitable to them, welcome them. For Derrida, 'hospitality' entails a willingness to be open to the other.[1] His notion of hospitality 'is ... firmly predicated on ... the possibility of encountering an unknown entity' (Kaufman 2001: 137). In other words when an 'unknown entity' is encountered we must greet it with an 'unquestioning welcome' (Derrida 2000: 29). Naas maintains that hospitality 'must remain, in its very conceptuality, an open question' (2003: 154). The knowledge economy cannot close itself off from the ghosts of alternative economies. To be inhospitable to ghosts may doom the knowledge economy to ignorance. Rather, it must remain open to something beyond itself. It may be disturbed by these ghosts' haunting presence, it may even fear confronting them. However, it must be hospitable to them nonetheless.

Note

1 'Hospitality' is a concept Derrida uses to discuss the ethical and political responsibility shown towards foreigners. He states 'hospitality demands that I open my "at home" and that I not only give to the stranger (devoid of last name, of a social status as stranger, etc.) but to the absolute, unknown, anonymous other, and that I *give him place*, that I let him come, that I let him arrive, and take place in the place that I offer to him, without asking him either for reciprocity (entering into a pact) or for his name' (2000: 29, original emphasis).

Appendix 1

We quote from a range of interviews we conducted with international senior staff members and Australian Commonwealth Government staff members, from the following organizations:

International

Education International
European Commission: Directorate General for Education and Culture
European Commission: Directorate General for Information Society
European Trade Union Committee for Education (ETUCE)
International Confederation of Free Trade Unions (ICFTU)
OECD: Centre for Educational Research and Innovation
Trade Union Advisory Committee (TUAC)
UNESCO: Communication and Information Sector
UNESCO: Higher Education Division

Australian Commonwealth Government

Access Branch, National Office of the Information Economy (NOIE)
Innovation and Industry Policy, Department of Industry, Tourism and Resources
Innovation and Research Branch, Higher Education Group, DEST
International Relations and Collaboration branch, Department of Education, Science and Training (DEST)
Science and Technology Policy branch, DEST
Stategy and Analysis branch, NOIE

Appendix 2

We use a number of different cameo studies that show a range of responses to, active engagements with, and contestations of, the manner in which knowledge economy policies are typically theorized.

Chapter 2 The risk economy

Research & Innovation enterprises at two universities in Australia (anonymized)
Tissue Culture & Art Project, University of Western Australia

Chapter 3 The gift economy

Online Open Access activism
Public knowledge projects associated with digital scholarly publications

Chapter 4 The libidinal economy

Andreas Gursky's photographs: *99 Cent* (1999) and *Siemens, Karlsruhe* (1991)
Christos Tsiolkas' novel: *Dead Europe* (2005)
Queensland University of Technology's creative industries project

Chapter 5 The survival economy

Captain Hook Awards
CSIRO's *Sustainable Ecosystems: Australian Native Foods* project
Desert Knowledge Australia website

Bibliography

Abrams, M. H. (1988) *A Glossary of Literary Terms*, fifth edition, Orlando, FL: Harcourt, Brace, Jovanovich.

Alberro, A. (2001) 'The Big Picture: blind ambition', *Art Forum*, 39(5): 104–14.

Aritho, G. M. (2001) 'Natural resource management: resolving contradiction between market and survival economies in Kenya', paper presented at the International Conference on Spatial Information for Sustainable Development, Nairobi, Kenya, October.

Association of Learned and Professional Society Publishers (ALPSP) (2005) *Dissemination of and access to UK research outputs: response from the Association of Learned and Professional Society Publishers (ALPSP) to the RCUK position paper*, ALPSP. Online. Available: www.alpsp.org/RCUK/Response.pdf (accessed 18 November 2005).

Association of Research Libraries (2003) *ARL Statistics*. Online. Available: www.arl.org/stats/arlstat (accessed 8 September 2005).

Australian Broadcasting Corporation (2001a) 'Ideas with wings (Part 3): million dollar labcoats', *Radio National: The Science Show*, 21 July. Online. Available: www.abc.net.au/rn/science/ss/stories/s327679.htm (accessed 7 September 2005).

——(2001b) 'Knowledge indignation: road rage on the information superhighway', *Radio National: Background Briefing*, 12 August. Online. Available: www.abc.net.au/rn/talks/bbing/stories/s345514.htm (accessed 8 September 2005).

Barry, P. (2002) *Beginning Theory: an introduction to literary and cultural theory*, second edition, Manchester: Manchester University Press.

Bataille, G. (1988) *The Accursed Share: an essay on general economy*, trans. Robert Hurley, New York: Zone Books.

Beck, U. (1992) *Risk Society: towards a new modernity*, trans. M. Ritter, London: Sage, first published 1986.

——(1994) 'The reinvention of politics: towards a theory of reflexive modernization', in U. Beck, A. Giddens and S. Lash (eds) *Reflexive Modernization: politics, tradition and aesthetics in the modern social order*, Cambridge: Polity.

——(1995) *Ecological Politics in the Age of Risk*, trans. Amos Weisz, Cambridge: Polity.

——(1996) 'Risk society and the provident state', in S. Lash, B. Szerszynski and B. Wynne (eds) *Risk, Environment and Modernity: towards a new ecology*, London: Sage.

——(1999) *World Risk Society*, Cambridge: Polity.

Beck, U., Giddens, A. and Lash, S. (eds) (1994) *Reflexive Modernization: politics, tradition and aesthetics in the modern social order*, Cambridge: Polity.

Bell, D. (1973) *The Coming of Post-Industrial Society: a venture in social forecasting*, New York: Basic Books.

——(1976) *The Coming of Post-Industrial Society: a venture in social forecasting*, New York: Basic Books, first published 1973.

——(1979) 'The social framework of the Information Society', in M. L. Dertouzos and J. Moses (eds) *The Computer Age: a twenty-year view*, Cambridge, MA: MIT Press.

Beniger, J. R. (1986) *The Control Revolution: technological and economic origins of the information society*, Cambridge, MA: Harvard University Press.

Berlin 3 Open Access (2005) *Progress in Implementing the Berlin Declaration on Open Access to Knowledge in the Sciences and Humanities*. Online. Available: www.eprints.org/events/berlin3/outcomes.html (accessed 18 November 2005).

Bernstein, J. M. (ed.) (1991) 'Introduction to T. Adorno', in *The Culture Industry: selected essays on mass culture*, London: Routledge.

Bethesda Statement on Open Access Publishing (2003), Maryland. Online. Available: www.earlham.edu/~peters/fos/bethesda.htm (accessed 8 September 2005).

Bimber, B. (1995) 'The three faces of technological determinism', in M. R. Smith and L. Marx (eds) *Does Technology Drive History? The dilemma of technological determinism*, Cambridge, MA: MIT Press.

Blair, T. (1998) *Our Competitive Future: building the knowledge-driven economy*, Cm 4176, London: Department of Trade and Industry.

Bluestone, B. and Harrison, B. (1982) *The Deindustrialization of America*, New York: Basic Books.

Böhme, G. and Stehr, N. (1986) *The Knowledge Society: the growing impact of scientific knowledge on social relations*, Dordrecht: D. Reidel Publishing Company.

Bollier, D. (2002) *Silent Theft: the private plunder of our common wealth*, London: Routledge.

Bourdieu, P. (1977) *Outline of a Theory of Practice*, trans. Richard Nice, Cambridge: Cambridge University Press.

Brint, S. (2001) 'Professionals and the "knowledge economy": rethinking the theory of postindustrial society', *Current Sociology*, 49(4): 101–32.

Brown, M. F. (2003) *Who Owns Native Culture?* Cambridge, MA: Harvard University Press.

Brown, N. and Michael, M. (2003) 'A sociology of expectations: retrospecting propects and prospecting', *Technology Analysis and Strategic Management*, 15: 3–19.

Bullen, E., Kenway, J. and Robb, S. (2004a) 'Can the arts and humanities survive the knowledge economy? A beginner's guide to the issues', in J. Kenway, E. Bullen and S. Robb (eds) *Innovation and Tradition: the arts, humanities and the knowledge economy*, New York: Peter Lang.

Bullen, E., Robb, S. and Kenway, J. (2004b) 'Creative destruction: knowledge economy policy and the future of the humanities and creative arts in the academy', *Journal of Education Policy*, 19(1): 3–22.

Bullen, E., Fahey, J. and Kenway, J. (2006) 'The knowledge economy and innovation: certain uncertainty in the risk economy', *Discourse: studies in the cultural politics of education*, 27(1): 53–68.

California Attorney General (2004) *Proposition 71: stem cell research, Funding. Bonds. Initiative constitutional amendment and statute*, Sacramento, CA: California Secretary of State. Online. Available: www.ss.ca.gov/elections/bp_nov04/prop_71_entire.pdf (accessed 7 September 2005).

Callari, A. (2002) 'The ghost of the gift: the unlikelihood of economics', in M. Osteen (ed.) *The Question of the Gift: essays across disciplines*, London: Routledge.

Captain Hook Awards (2005) *Website*. Online. Available: www.captain hookawards.org/history.html (accessed 28 November 2005).

Carrick, D. (2004) 'The estate of James Joyce; the Free Trade Agreement; and some contemporary conundrums', *Radio National: The Law Report*, 14 September. Online. Available: www.abc.net.au/rn/talks/8.30/lawrpt/stories/s1198816.htm (accessed 5 December 2005).

Carrier, J. G. (1995) *Gifts and Commodities: exchange and western capitalism since 1700*, London: Routledge.

Carroll, N. (1998) *A Philosophy of Mass Art*, Oxford: Oxford University Press.

Castells, M. (1996a) *The Rise of the Network Society*, Oxford: Blackwell.

——(1996b) 'The Net and the self', *Critique of Anthropology*, 16(1): 9–38.

Catts, O. (2002) 'Bio-feel statement', *Bio-feel*, Biennale of Electronic Arts, Perth, August. Online. Available: www.tca.uwa.edu.au/biofeel/statment.html (accessed 17 January 2003).

Catts, O. and Zurr, I. (2002) 'Growing semi-living sculptures: the tissue culture and art project', *Leonardo*, 35(4): 365–70.

Caves, R. (2000) *Creative Industries: contracts between art and commerce*, Cambridge, MA: Harvard University Press.

Cerny, L. (1997–98) 'Dickens' *A Christmas Carol*: revisiting and reformation', *Connotations*, 7(3): 255–72.

Cheal, D. (1988) *The Gift Economy*, London: Routledge.

Commonwealth of Australia (2001) *Backing Australia's Ability: an innovation action plan for the future*, Canberra: AGPS.

——(2004) *Backing Australia's Ability – Building our Future through Science and Innovation*, Canberra: AGPS.

Commonwealth Science and Research Organisation (CSIRO) (2003) *Flu Cure: Australia Advances, Series Six*. Online. Available: www.csiro.au/promos/ozadvances/series6flucure.html (accessed 7 September 2005).

——(2005) *Sustainable Ecosystems Program*. Online. Available: www.cse.csiro.au/index.htm (accessed 26 November 2005).

Cooper, B. P. and Murphy, M. S. (1999) 'Libidinal Economies: Lyotard and accounting for the unaccountable', in M. Woodmansee and M. Osteen (eds) *New Economic Criticism: studies at the intersection of literature and economics*, London: Routledge.

CORDIS (2002) *Innovation policy background; Innovation policy: Studies*. Online. Available: www.cordis.lu/innovation-policy/studies/home.html (accessed 7 September 2005).

Critchley, S. (1995) 'On Derrida's *Specters of Marx*', *Philosophy and Social Criticism*, 21(3): 1–30.

Crow, R. (2002) *SPARC Institutional Repository Checklist and Resource Guide*, Washington DC: Scholarly Publishing and Academic Resources Coalition.

Cullenberg, S., Amariglio, J. and Ruccio, D. F. (eds) (2001) *Postmodernism, Economics and Knowledge*, London and New York: Routledge.
Cunningham, S. (2001) 'From cultural to creative industries: theory, industry and policy implications', in C. Mercer (ed.) *Culturelink Review*, Zagreb, Croatia: Institute for International Relations.
—— (2002) 'Culture, services, knowledge or is content king, or are we just drama queens?' paper presented at Communications Research Forum, Canberra, Australia, October.
Cunningham, S. and Hartley, J. (2001) 'Creative industries – from Blue Poles to fat pipes', in M. Gillies (ed.) *The National Humanities and Social Sciences Summit: position papers*, Canberra: DEST.
Daly, H. E. (1994) 'Operationalizing sustainable development by investing in natural capital', in A. Jansson, M. Hammer, C. Folke and R. Costanza (eds) *Investing in Natural Capital*, Washington, DC: Island Press.
——(1997) 'Uneconomic growth: from empty-world to full-world economics', in J. Schmandt, C. H. Ward and B. Alberts (eds) *Sustainable Development: the challenge of transition*, Cambridge: Cambridge University Press.
——(1998) 'Beyond growth: avoiding uneconomic growth', paper presented at International Society for Ecological Economies, 5th Biennial Conference, Santiago, Chile, November.
David, P. A. and Foray, D. (2003) 'Economic fundamentals of the knowledge society', *Policy Futures in Education*, 1(1): 20–49.
Department for Culture, Media and Sport (DCMS) (1998) *Creative Industries Mapping Document*. Online. Available: www.culture.gov.uk/global/publications/archive_1998/Creative_Industries_Mapping_Document_1998.htm (accessed 23 July 2005).
——(2001) *Culture and Creativity: the next ten years*. Online. Available: www.culture.gov.uk/global/publications/archive_2001/Culture_Creativity10yrs.htm (accessed 23 July 2005).
Department of Education, Science and Training (DEST) (2000) *Learning for the knowledge society: an education and training action plan for the information economy*, Canberra: Commonwealth of Australia. Online. Available: www.detya.gov.au/edu/edactplan.htm (accessed 6 September 2005).
Department of Industry, Science and Resources (ISR) (1999) *Shaping Australia's Future: innovation – framework paper*, Canberra: Department of Industry, Science and Resources.
Department of Trade and Industry (DTI) (UK) (2000) *Excellence and Opportunity – a science and innovation policy for the 21st century*. Online. Available: www.ost.gov.uk/enterprise/excellence.htm (accessed 7 September 2005).
——(2003) *Competing in the Global Economy: the innovation challenge*, London, UK Government. Online. Available: www.dti.gov.uk/innovation report/innovation-report-full.pdf (accessed 14 July 2005).
——(2005) *Innovation Report: competing in the global economy: the innovation challenge*, London: Department of Trade and Industry. Online. Available: www.innovation.gov.uk/innovationreport (accessed 8 August 2005).
Derrida, J. (1976) *Of Grammatology*, trans. Gayatri Chakravorty Spivak, Baltimore, MD: Johns Hopkins University Press.
——(1992a) 'Force of law: the "mystical foundation of authority"', in D. Cornell,

M. Rosenfeld and D. G. Carlson (eds) *Deconstruction and the Possibility of Justice*, London: Routledge.

——(1992b) *The Other Heading: reflections on today's Europe*, translated by P.-A. Brault and M. B. Naas, Bloomington, IN: Indiana University Press.

——(1992c) *Given Time. I, Counterfeit money*, trans. Peggy Kamuf, Chicago, IL: University of Chicago Press.

——(1994) *Specters of Marx: the state of the debt, the work of mourning, and the New International*, trans. Peggy Kamuf, New York: Routledge.

——(1998) *I distrust the Utopia, I want the Impossible: interview with Thomas Assheuer*, Die Ziet, 11. Online. Available: http://culturemachine.tees.ac.uk/Cmach/Backissues/j002/Articles/art_derr.htm (accessed 6 September 2005).

——(2000) *Of Hospitality: Anne Dufourmantelle invites Jacques Derrida to respond*, Stanford, CA: Stanford University Press.

Dertouzos, M. L. and Moses, J. (eds) (1979) *The Computer Age: a twenty-year view*, Cambridge, MA: MIT Press.

Desert Knowledge Australia (2005) Website. Online. Available: www.desert knowledge.com.au/dka/index.cfm?fuseaction=aboutus (accessed 25 November 2005).

Dickens, C. ([1843] 2003) *A Christmas Carol and other Christmas Writing*, London: Penguin, first published 1843.

DIPEx (2005) Online. Available: www.dipex.org/main.asp (accessed 1 August 2005).

Dizard, W. P. (1982) *The Coming Information Age: an overview of technology, economics and politics*, New York: Longman.

Douglas, M. and Wildavsky, A. (1982) *Risk and Culture: an essay on the selection of technical and environmental dangers*, Berkeley, CA: University of California Press.

Drahos, P. (1996) *A Philosophy of Intellectual Property*, Applied Legal Philosophy Series, Dartmouth: Aldershot.

Drahos, P. and Braithwaite, J. (2002) *Information Feudalism: who owns the knowledge economy?* London: Earthscan.

Drucker, P. F. (1959) *Landmarks of Tomorrow*, New York: Harper & Brothers.

——(1969) *The Age of Discontinuity: guidelines to our changing society*, New York: Harper & Row.

——(1993) *Post-capitalist Society*, Oxford: Butterworth-Heinemann.

du Gay, P. (2004) 'Against enterprise (but not against "enterprise"), for that would make no sense', *Organization*, 11: 37–57.

Dyer-Witheford, N. (1999) *Cyber-Marx: cycles and circuits of struggle in high-technology capitalism*, Urbana, IL: University of Illinois Press.

Elam, M. (1994) 'Puzzling out the post-Fordist debate: technology, markets, institutions', in A. Amin (ed.) *Post-Fordism: a reader*, Oxford: Blackwell.

Elliot, A. (2002) 'Beck's sociology of risk: a critical assessment', *Sociology*, 36(2): 293–315.

Epstein, D., Kenway, J. and Boden, R. (2005) *Academic Support Kit: writing for publication*, London: Sage.

Erosion Technology and Concentration Group (ETC Group) (2004) *From Global Enclosure to Self Enclosure: ten years after – a critique of the CBD and the 'Bonn Guidelines' on access and benefit sharing (ABS)* Communiqué, Issue 83, January/February.

——(2005) Homepage. Online. Available: www.etcgroup.org/key_defs.asp (accessed 21 November 2005).
European Commission (1995) *Teaching and Learning – Towards the Learning Society*, COM(95)590: European Commission. Online. Available: http://europa.eu.int/comm/education/doc/official/keydoc/lb-en.pdf (accessed 7 September 2005).
——(2000) *Challenges for Enterprise Policy in the Knowledge-driven Economy: proposal for a Council decision on a multiannual programme for enterprise and entrepreneurship (2001–2005)*, COM(2000) 256 final/2, Brussels: Commission of the European Communities.
——(2002a) *Towards a Knowledge-based Europe: the European Union and the information society*, Luxembourg: European Commission. Online. Available: http://europa.eu.int/information_society/newsroom/documents/catalogue_en.pdf (accessed 6 September 2005).
——(2002b) *Participating in European Research: sixth framework programme*, Luxembourg: Office for Official Publications of the European Communities.
——(2002c) *The EU at the WSSD: EU focus on global public goods*. Online. Available: http://europa.eu.int/comm/environment/wssd/publicgoods.pdf (accessed 7 September 2005).
——(2003a) *Choosing to Grow: knowledge, innovation and jobs in a cohesive society*, report to the Spring European Council, 21 March on the Lisbon strategy of economic, social and environmental renewal, Luxembourg: Office for Official Publications of the European Communities.
——(2003b) *Knowledge Society – Homepage*. Online. Available: http://europa.eu.int/comm/employment_social/knowledge_society/index_en.htm (accessed 30 September 2003).
——(2005a) *Building the ERA of Knowledge for Growth*, COM (2005) 118 final, Brussels: European Commission.
——(2005b) *European Commission Study on the Economic and Technical Evolution of Scientific Publication Markets in Europe*. Online. Available: www.europa.eu.int/comm/research/press/2004/pr1506en.cfm (accessed 8 September 2005).
Fagerberg, J. (2002) 'A layman's guide to evolutionary economics', Industrial R&D and Innovation Policy Learning, 18–19 April, Leangkollen, Asker. Online. Available: http://folk.uio.no/janf/downloadp/02fagerberg_evolution.pdf (accessed 16 July 2004).
Fahey, J. (2004) *David Noonan: before and now*, Melbourne, Australia: Thames and Hudson.
Fahey, J., Bullen, E. and Kenway, J. (2005) 'A Taste for Science: inventing the young in the national interest', in D. Bell and J. Hollows (eds) *Ordinary Lifestyles: popular media, consumption and taste*, Buckingham, UK: Open University Press.
Fahey, J., Kenway, J., Bullen, E. and Robb, S. (2006) 'Knowledge beyond the knowledge economy: merely cultural: merely commercial? Merely civilising?', in J. Ozga, T. S. Popkewitz and T. Seddon (eds) *World Yearbook of Education 2006: education research and policy volume*, London: Kogan Page.
Featherstone, M. (1992) *Consumer Culture and Postmodernism*, London: Sage.
Federal Trade Commission [USA] (2003) *Competition and Intellectual Property Law and Policy in the Knowledge-Based Economy*, Washington DC: Federal Trade Commission.
Fennell, L. A. (2002) 'Unpacking the gift: illiquid goods and empathetic dialogue', in

M. Osteen (ed.) *The Question of the Gift: essays across disciplines*, London: Routledge.
Florida, R. (2003) *The Rise of the Creative Class: and how it's transforming work, leisure, community and everyday life*, New York: Basic Books.
Foucault, M. (1973) *The Birth of the Clinic: an archaeology of medical perception*, London: Tavistock.
Fournier, V. and Grey, C. (1999) 'Too much, too little and too often: a critique of du Gay's analysis of enterprise', *Organization*, 6: 107–28.
Freeman, C. (1987) *Technology Policy and Economic Performance: lessons from Japan*, London: Pinter.
Freeman, C. and Louçã, F. (2001) *As Time Goes By: from the industrial revolutions to the information revolution*, Oxford: Oxford University Press.
Freeman, C. and Perez, C. (1988) 'Structural crises of adjustment, business cycles and investment behaviour', in G. Dosi, C. Freeman, R. Nelson, G. Silverberg and L. Soete (eds) *Technical Change and Economic Theory*, London: Pinter.
Freeman, C., Clark, J. and Soete, L. (1982) *Unemployment and Technical Innovation: a study of long waves and economic development*, London: Pinter.
Frow, J. (1997) *Time and Commodity Culture*, Oxford: Clarendon Press.
Fukuyama, F. (1992) *The End of History and the Last Man*, New York: HarperCollins.
Ghelfi, D. (2005) *Understanding the Engine of Creativity in a Creative Economy: An interview with John Howkins*, World Intellectual Property Organisation. Online. Available: www.wipo.int/sme/en/documents/cr_interview_howkins.html# (accessed 19 September 2005).
Gibbons, M. (1998) *Higher education relevance in the 21st century*, Online. Available: www-wds.worldbank.org/servlet/WDS_IBank_Servlet?pcont =details&eid=000094946_9912220532351 (accessed 5 September 2005).
Gibbons, M., Limoges, C., Nowotny, H., Schwartzman, S., Scott, P. and Trow, M. (1994) *The New Production of Knowledge: the dynamics of science and research in contemporary societies*, London: Sage.
Giddens, A. (1991) *Modernity and Self Identity: self and society in the late modern age*, Cambridge: Polity.
——(1994) 'Living in a post-traditional society', in U. Beck, A. Giddens and S. Lash (eds) *Reflexive Modernization: politics, tradition and aesthetics in the modern social order*, Cambridge: Polity.
——(1999) *Risk [Lecture 2]*, BBC Reith Lectures: Runaway World. Online. Available: http://news.bbc.co.uk/hi/english/static/events/reith_99/week2/week2.htm (accessed 6 September 2005).
Gouldner, A. (1979) *The Future of Intellectuals and the Rise of the New Class*, London: Macmillan.
Government of Canada (2002) *Knowledge Matters: skills and learning for Canadians*, Hull: Human Resources Development Canada. Online. Available: www.innovationstrategy.gc.ca (accessed 1 September 2005).
Government of Ireland (2005) *Ireland now a Knowledge Economy*. Online. Available: www.idaireland.com/home/index.aspx?id=625 (accessed 1 September 2005).
Gregory, C. A. (1982) *Gifts and Commodities*, London: Academic.
Grierson, E. M. (2003) 'The Arts and Creative Industries: new alliances in the humanities', paper presented at Hawaii International Conference on Arts and Humanities, Waikiki Hotel, Hawaii, February.

Group of Eight (2004) *Statement on Open Access to Scholarly Information.* Online. Available: www.go8.edu.au/news/2004/Go8%20Statement%20on%20open%20access%20to%20scholarly%20information%20May%20%85.pdf (accessed 8 September 2005).

Hall, S. and Jacques, M. (eds) (1990) *New Times: the changing face of politics in the 1990s*, London: Verso, first published 1989.

Hart, S. L. (1997) 'Beyond Greening: strategies for a sustainable world', *Harvard Business Review*, January–February: 66–76.

Hart, S. L. and Milstein, M. B. (1999) 'Global sustainability and the creative destruction of industries', *Sloan Management Review*, Fall: 23–33.

Hartley, J. (2004) 'Preface', in R. Wissler, B. Haseman, S.-A. Wallace and M. Keane (eds) *Innovation in Australian Arts, Media, Design: fresh challenges for the tertiary sector*, Flaxton, QLD: Post Pressed.

Hartley, J., Cunningham, S., Hearn, G. and Jones, J. (2002) *Response to the Queensland R&D Strategy Issues Paper*, Queensland, Australia: Creative Industries Faculty, Queensland University of Technology.

Harvey, D. (1989) *The Condition of Postmodernity: an enquiry into the origins of cultural change*, Oxford: Blackwell.

Hawken, P., Lovins, A. and Hunter Lovins, L. (1999) *Natural Capitalism: creating the next industrial revolution*, Boston, MA: Little, Brown.

Hayek, F. (1937) *Economics and Knowledge; Economica IV*. Online. Available: www.virtualschool.edu/mon/Economics/HayekEconomicsAndKnowledge.html (accessed 5 September 2005).

——(1945) 'The use of knowledge in society', *American Economic Review*, 35(4): 519–30.

Henry, M., Lingard, B., Rizvi, F. and Taylor, S. (2001) *The OECD, Globalisation and Education Policy*, Oxford: IAU Press/Pergamon.

Hesmondhalgh, D. (2002) *The Cultural Industries*, London: Sage.

Holton, R. J. (1992) *Economy and Society*, London: Routledge.

Horkheimer, M. and Adorno, T. W. (1973) *Dialectic of Enlightenment*, London: Allen Lane.

Howitt, P. (2000) 'Endogenous growth and cross-country income differences', *American Economic Review*, 90: 829–46.

Howkins, J. (2001) *The Creative Economy: how people make money from ideas*, London: Penguin.

Humphery, K. (1998) *Shelf Life: supermarkets and the changing cultures of consumption*, Cambridge: Cambridge University Press.

Hyde, L. (1983) *The Gift: imagination and the erotic life of property*, New York: Random.

Innis, H. (1951) *The Bias of Communication*, Toronto: University of Toronto Press.

Irwin, A. and Wynne, B. (eds) (1996) *Misunderstanding Science? The public reconstruction of science and technology*, Cambridge: Cambridge University Press.

James, W. and Allen, N. J. (eds) (1998) *Marcel Mauss: a centenary tribute*, New York: Berghahn.

Jameson, F. (1984) 'Postmodernism or the cultural logic of late capitalism', *New Left Review*, 146: 59–92.

——(1995) 'Marx's purloined letter: on Derrida and Marx', *New Left Review*, 209: 75–109.

Jessop, B. (2000) *The State and the Contradictions of the Knowledge-driven Economy*, Lancaster: Department of Sociology, Lancaster University. Online. Available: www.comp.lancs.ac.uk/sociology/soc044rj.html (accessed 12 July 2005).

Johnson, R. K. (2004) 'Open Access: unlocking the value of scientific research', paper presented at The New Challenge for Research Libraries: collection management and strategic access to digital resources, Oklahoma, March.

Jones, B. (1995) *Sleepers, Wake! Technology and the future of work*, Melbourne: Oxford University Press, first published 1982.

Joseph, J. (2001) 'Derrida's spectres of ideology', *Journal of Political Ideologies*, 6(1): 95–115.

Kaufman, E. (2001) *The Delirium of Praise: Bataille, Blanchot, Derrida, Foucault, Klossowski*, Baltimore, MD: Johns Hopkins University Press.

Kaul, I., Grunberg, I. and Stern, M. A. (1999) 'Defining global public goods', in I. Kaul, I. Grunberg and M. Stern (eds) *Global Public Goods: international cooperation in the 21st Century*, Oxford and New York: Oxford University Press.

Kemp, D. (1999) *Knowledge and Innovation: a policy statement on research and research training*, Canberra: Commonwealth of Australia.

Kenway, J. and Bullen, E. (2005) 'Globalising the young in the age of desire: some educational policy issues', in M. Apple, J. Kenway and M. Singh (eds) *Globalizing Public Education: policies, pedagogies and politics*, New York: Peter Lang.

Kenway, J. and Langmead, D. (2002) 'Is there a future for feminism in the contemporary university?', in C. Reynolds (ed.) *Women and Leadership: questions at the cutting edge*, Albany, NY: SUNY Press.

Kenway, J., Bullen, E. and Robb, S. (2004a) 'The knowledge economy, the technopreneur and the problematic future of the university', *Policy Futures in Education*, 2: 330–49.

—— (eds) (2004b) *Innovation and Tradition: the arts, humanities and the knowledge economy*, New York: Peter Lang.

—— (2004c) 'Global knowledge politics and "exploitable knowledge"', in J. Kenway, E. Bullen and S. Robb (eds) *Innovation and Tradition: the arts, humanities, and the knowledge economy*, New York: Peter Lang.

Kerr, C. (1963) *The Uses of the University*, Cambridge, MA: Harvard University Press.

Keynes, J. M. (1937) 'The general theory of employment', *Quarterly Journal of Economics*, 51: 209–23.

Khor, M. (2004) *A Worldwide Fight Against Biopiracy and Patents on Life*. Online. Available: www.twnside.org.sg/title/pat-ch.htm (accessed 29 November 2005).

—— (2005) *WIPO to Convene Meetings on 'Development Agenda'*. Online. Available: www.twnside.otg.sg/title2/twr171b.htm (accessed 21 November 2005).

Kirzner, I. M. (1984) 'The role of the entrepreneur in the economic system', paper presented at The Inaugural John Bonython Lecture, Adelaide, July. Online. Available: www.cis.org.au/Events/JBL/jbl84.htm (accessed 7 September 2005).

Knight, F. (1921) *Risk, Uncertainty, and Profit*, Boston, MA: Hart, Schaffner & Marx; Houghton Mifflin Company.

Knight, J. (2004) *California Says "Yes" to Stem-cell Research*. Online. Available: http://npg.nature.com/news/2004/041101/full/041101-11.html (accessed 7 September 2005).

Komter, A. (ed.) (1996) *The Gift: an interdisciplinary perspective*, Amsterdam: Amsterdam University Press.
Krimsky, S. (2003) *Science in the Private Interest: has the lure of profits corrupted biomedical research?* Lanham, MD: Rowman & Littlefield.
—— (2004) *Science in the Private Interest: has the lure of profits corrupted biomedical research?* Lanham, MD: Rowman & Littlefield, new edition.
Kundnani, A. (1998–99) 'Where do you want to go today? The rise of information capital', *Race and Class*, 40(2–3): 49–72.
Laclau, E. (1995) 'The time is out of joint', *Diacritics*, 25(2): 86–96.
Laidlaw, J. (2002) 'A free gift makes no friends', in M. Osteen (ed.) *The Question of the Gift: essays across disciplines*, London: Routledge.
Lamberton, D. M. (1974) *The Information Revolution*, Philadelphia, PA: American Academy of Political and Social Sciences.
Lane, R. E. (1966) 'The decline of politics and ideology in a knowledgeable society', *American Sociological Review*, 31: 649–62.
Lash, S. (1994) 'Reflexivity and its doubles: structure, aesthetics, community', in U. Beck, A. Giddens and S. Lash (eds) *Reflexive Modernization: politics, traditions and aesthetics in the modern social order*, Cambridge: Polity.
Lash, S. and Urry, J. (1987) *The End of Organized Capitalism*, Cambridge: Polity.
—— (1994) *Economies of Signs and Space*, London: Sage.
Lash, S. and Wynne, B. (1992) 'Introduction', in U. Beck (ed.) *Risk Society: towards a new modernity*, London: Sage.
Leadbeater, C. (1999) *Living on Thin Air: The New Economy*, London: Penguin.
Lee, M. J. (2000) *The Consumer Society Reader*, Oxford: Blackwell.
Lévi-Strauss, C. (1987) 'Introduction', in *Works of Marcel Mauss*, trans. Felicity Baker, London: Routledge & Kegan Paul.
Lowe, I. (2005) *A Big Fix: radical solutions for Australia's environmental crisis*, Melbourne, Australia: Black Inc.
Lucy, N. (2004) *A Derrida Dictionary*, Malden, MA: Blackwell.
Luhmann, N. (1993) *Risk: a sociological analysis*, New York: Aldine de Gruyter.
Lundvall, B.-Å. (1998) 'The learning economy – implications for the knowledge base of health and education systems', paper presented at High-Level Seminar on Production, Mediation and Use of Knowledge in the Education and Health Sectors, Paris, May.
Lundvall, B.-Å. and Archibugi, D. (2001a) 'Introduction: Europe and the learning economy', in B.-Å. Lundvall and D. Archibugi (eds) *The Globalizing Learning Economy*, Oxford: Oxford University Press.
—— (2001b) 'Innovation policy in the globalizing learning economy', in B.-Å. Lundvall and D. Archibugi (eds) *The Globalizing Learning Economy*, Oxford: Oxford University Press.
Lundvall, B.-Å. and Johnson, B. (1994) 'The learning economy', *Journal of Industry Studies*, 1(2): 23–42.
Lupton, D. (1999) *Risk*, London: Routledge.
Lyon, D. (1991) *The Information Society: issues and illusions*, Cambridge: Polity, first published 1988.
Lyotard, J.-F. (1984) *The Postmodern Condition: a report on knowledge*, Manchester: Manchester University Press.
—— (1989) *The Lyotard Reader*, Oxford: Blackwell.

——(1993) *Libidinal Economy*, trans. Iain Hamilton Grant, Bloomington, IN: Indiana University Press, first published 1974.

McDonald, D. (1957) 'A theory of mass culture', in B. Rosenberg and D. Manning White (eds) *Mass Culture: the popular arts in America*, New York: The Free Press.

Machlup, F. (1962) *The Production and Distribution of Knowledge in the United States*, Princeton, NJ: Princeton University Press.

McQueen, H. (2005) 'Dead Europe: review'. Online. Available: www.alphalink.com.au/~loge27/literature/lit_dead_europe.htm (accessed 15 September 2005).

McRobbie, A. (2002) 'Clubs to companies: notes on the decline of political culture in speeded up creative worlds', *Cultural Studies*, 16(4): 516–31.

Magnus, B. and Cullenberg, S. (1994) 'Editors' Introduction', in J. Derrida *Specters of Marx: the state of the debt, the work of mourning, and the New International*, trans. Peggy Kamuf, New York: Routledge.

Malaguerra, C., Niklowitz, M. and Huber, M. (2001) 'Monitoring the Information Society', paper presented at IAOS Satellite Meeting on Statistics for the Information Society, Tokyo, August.

Manne, R. (2005) 'Dead disturbing', *The Monthly*, June: 50–3.

Marginson, S. (2002) 'What's wrong with the universities?', *Arena Magazine*, 61: BB3–BB16.

Martin, J. and Butler, D. (1981) *Viewdata and the Information Society*, Englewood Cliffs, NJ: Prentice-Hall.

Martin, W. J. (1988) *The Information Society*, London: Aslib.

Marx, K. (1915) 'Part one: Commodities and money; Chapter one: Commodities', in F. Engels (ed.) *Capital: a critique of political economy*, Chicago: Charles H. Kerr, first published 1867.

——([1859] 1971) *A Contribution to the Critique of Political Economy*, Moscow: Progress Publishers, first published 1859.

Marx, K. and Engels, F. ([1848] 2002) *The Communist Manifesto*, London: Penguin, first published 1848.

Masuda, Y. (1972) *Social Impact of Computerization: an application pattern for industrial society*, Tokyo: Kondansha.

——(1976) *Information Economics*, Tokyo: Sangyo Noritsu University Press.

——(1980) *The Information Society as Post-industrial Society*, Washington DC: World Futures Society.

Mauss, M. ([1925] 1990) *The Gift: the form and reason for exchange in archaic societies*, trans. W. D. Halls, New York: W. W. Norton, first published 1925.

Max Planck Society (2003) *Berlin Declaration on Open Access to Knowledge in the Sciences and Humanities*, Berlin. Online. Available: www.zim.mpg.de/openacess-berlin/berlindeclaration.html (accessed 8 September 2005).

May, C. (2000) 'Feature review: living on thin air', *New Political Economy*, 5(1): 145–8.

——(2002) *The Information Society: a sceptical view*, Cambridge: Polity.

MICA (Ministry of Information, Communication and the Arts) (Singapore) (2005) *Creative Industries*. Online. Available: www.mica.gov.sg/mica_business/b_creative.html (accessed 14 September 2005).

Mirowski, P. (2001) 'Refusing the gift', in S. Cullenberg, J. Amariglio and D. F. Ruccio (eds) *Postmodernism, Economics and Knowledge*, London: Routledge.

Mitchell, D. (1999) *Governmentality: power and rule in modern society*, London: Sage.

Morris-Suzuki, T. (1988) *Beyond Computopia: information, automation and democracy in Japan*, London: Kegan Paul.

Naas, M. (2003) *Taking on the Tradition: Jacques Derrida and the legacies of deconstruction*, Cultural Memory in the Present, Stanford, CA: Stanford University Press.

Naisbitt, J. (1984) *Megatrends: ten new directions transforming our lives*, London: MacDonald.

Neef, R. (2002) 'Aspects of the informal economy in a transforming country: the case of Romania', *International Journal of Urban and Regional Research*, 26(2): 299–322.

Nora, S. and Minc, A. (1978) *L'informatisation de la Société*, Paris: La Documentation Francaise.

Nowotny, H., Scott, P. and Gibbons, M. (2003) 'Introduction: Mode 2: Revisited: the new production of knowledge', *Minerva*, 41(3): 179–94.

Organisation for Economic Co-operation and Development (OECD) (1996) *The Knowledge-based Economy*, Paris: OECD.

——(1999a) *Managing National Innovation Systems*, Paris: OECD.

——(1999b) *Boosting Innovation: the cluster approach*, Paris: OECD.

——(2001a) *Innovative Clusters: drivers of national innovation systems*, Paris: OECD.

——(2001b) *Innovative Networks: co-operation in national innovation systems*, Paris: OECD.

——(2001c) *Innovative People: mobility of skilled personnel in national innovation systems*, Paris: OECD.

——(2003) *Creativity, Innovation and Economic Growth in the 21st Century: an affirmative case for intellectual property rights*, Paris: OECD.

——(2004a) *Innovation in the Knowledge Economy: implications for education and learning*, Paris: Centre for Educational Research and Innovation.

——(2004b) *Declaration on Access to Research Data from Public Funding*. Online. Available: www.oecd.org/document/0,2340,en_2649_34487_25998799_1_1_1_1,00.html (accessed 8 September 2005).

Ohlin, A. (2002) 'Andreas Gursky and the contemporary sublime', *Art Journal*, 61(4), Winter: 22–33.

Ong, A. and Collier, S. J. (2005) *Global Assemblages: technology, politics and ethics as anthropological problems*, Malden, MA: Blackwell.

Open Society Institute (2002) *Budapest Open Access Initiative*, Budapest. Online. Available: www.soros.org/openaccess/read.shtml (accessed 8 September 2005).

Open Source Initiative (OSI) (2005) *Open Source*. Online. Available: www.opensource.org (accessed 8 September 2005).

Osteen, M. (2002a) 'Gift or commodity?', in M. Osteen (ed.) *The Question of the Gift: essays across disciplines*, London: Routledge.

——(ed.) (2002b) *The Question of the Gift: essays across disciplines*, London: Routledge.

Patton, P. (2004) 'Politics', in J. Reynolds and J. Roffe (eds) *Understanding Derrida*, New York: Continuum.

Pearson, H. (2004) 'Science suffers in race for "scoops"', *The Weekend Australian*, 17–18 January, Health Section: 4.

Perez, C. (1983) 'Structural change and the assimilation of new technologies in the economic and social system', *Futures*, 15(5): 357–75.

——(1985) 'Microelectronics, long waves and world structural system: new perspectives for developing countries', *World Development*, 13: 441–63.
Peters, M. (2001) 'National education policy constructions of the "knowledge economy": towards a critique', *Journal of Educational Enquiry*, 2(1): 1–22.
——(2003a) 'Classical political economy and the role of universities in the new knowledge economy', *Globalisation, Societies and Education*, 1(2): 153–68.
——(2003b) 'Education in the knowledge economy', *Policy Futures in Education*, 1(1): 1–19.
Piore, M. and Sabel, C. (1984) *The Second Industrial Divide*, New York: Basic Books.
Polanyi, K. (1977) *The Livelihood of Man*, New York: Academic Press.
Polanyi, M. (1958) *Personal Knowledge*, London: Routledge & Kegan Paul.
——(1966) *The Tacit Dimension*, London: Routledge & Kegan Paul.
Porat, M. U. (1977) *The Information Economy: definition and measurement*, Washington DC: U.S. Department of Commerce, Office of Telecommunications.
Public Knowledge Project (2005) *What is the Public Knowledge Project?*, British Columbia, University of British Columbia. Online. Available: www.pkp.ubc.ca/about/what.html (accessed 17 July 2005).
Queensland University of Technology (QUT) (2004) *Creative Industries*, Brisbane, Australia: QUT.
Readings, B. (1991) *Introducing Lyotard: art and politics*, London: Routledge.
Reddy, S. G. (1996) 'Claims to expert knowledge and the subversion of democracy: the triumph of risk over uncertainty', *Economy and Society*, 25: 222–54.
Research Councils UK (RCUK) (2005) *Research Councils UK, Position Statement on Access to Research Outputs*, London: RCUK. Online. Available: www.rcuk.ac.uk/access/index.asp (accessed 8 September 2005).
Rifkin, J. (2000) *The Age of Access: the new culture of hypercapitalism where all of life is a paid-for experience*, New York: Putnam.
Rivkin, J. and Ryan, M. (2004) *Literary Theory: an anthology*, Malden, MA: Blackwell.
Robb, S. and Bullen, E. (2004) 'A provocation', in J. Kenway, E. Bullen and S. Robb (eds) *Innovation and Tradition: the arts, humanities and the knowledge economy*, New York: Peter Lang.
Robb, S., Bullen, E. and Kenway, J. (2003) 'So young and enterprising: the knowledge economy in Australian schools', in A. Reid and P. Thomson (eds) *Rethinking Public Education: a conversation*. Queensland: Redress Press and Australian Curriculum Studies Association.
Romer, P. M. (1986) 'Increasing returns and long run growth', *Journal of Political Economy*, 94(5): 1002–37.
——(1990) 'Endogenous technological change', *Journal of Political Economy*, 98(5): 71–102.
Rooney, D., Hearn, G., Mandeville, T. and Joseph, R. (2003) *Public Policy in Knowledge Based Economies: foundations and frameworks*, Cheltenham, UK: Edward Elgar.
Rose, N. (1998) *Inventing Ourselves: psychology, power, personhood*, Cambridge: Cambridge University Press.
——(2005) 'Will biomedicine transform society?', *Radio National: Background Briefing*, 13 March. Online. Available: www.abc.net.au/rn/talks/bbing/stories/s1323567.htm (accessed 29 November 2005).

Roszak, T. (1986) *The Cult of Information: the folklore of computers and the true art of thinking*, New York: Pantheon.

Sangyo Kozo Shingikai Joho Sangyo Bukai (1969) 'Nihon Shakai Johoka Sokushin no tame no Seisaku Yoko (Policy outlines for promoting the informization of Japanese society)', *Ekonomisuto* (June): 53–6 (summary).

Schoenberger, E. (1987) 'Technological and organisational change in automobile production: spatial implications', *Regional Studies*, 21(3): 199–214.

——(1988) 'From Fordism to flexible accumulation: technology, competitive strategies and international locations', *Environment and Planning D: Society and Space*, 6(3): 245–62.

Scholarly Publishing and Academic Resources Coalition (SPARC) (2005) *Open Access Newsletter*, Issue No. 87. Online. Available: www.earlham.edu/~peters/fos/newsletter/07-02-05.htm (accessed 8 September 2005).

Schrift, A. D. (ed.) (1997) *The Logic of the Gift: toward an ethic of generosity*, London: Routledge.

Schumpeter, J. A. (1939) *Business Cycles: a theoretical, historical, and statistical analysis of the capitalist process*, New York: McGraw-Hill.

——(1943) *Capitalism, Socialism and Democracy*, New York: Harper & Brothers.

——([1934] 1978) *The Theory of Economic Development: an inquiry into profits, capital, credit interest, and the business cycle*, Oxford: Oxford University Press, first published 1934.

Seares, M. (2001) 'National Press Club Address', Canberra, Australia: National Press Club.

Shannon, C. and Weaver, W. (1964) *The Mathematical Theory of Communication*, Urbana, IL: University of Illinois Press, first published 1949.

Shiva, V. (1993) *Monocultures of the Mind: perspectives on biodiversity and biotechnology*, London: Zed Books; Penang: Third World Network.

——(1997) *Biopiracy: the plunder of nature and knowledge*, Cambridge, MA: South End Press.

——(1999) 'The US patent system legalizes theft and biopiracy', July 28, *The Hindu*, Madras. Online. Available: www.organicconsumers.org/Patent/uspatsys.cfm (accessed 29 November 2005).

——(2000a) *Tomorrow's Biodiversity*, London: Thames and Hudson.

——(2000b) *Stolen Harvest: the hijacking of the global food supply*, Cambridge, MA: South End Press.

——(2000c) *Poverty and Globalisation*, BBC Reith Lectures: Respect for the Earth. Online. Available: http://news.bbc.co.uk/hi/english/static/events/reith_2000/lecture5.stm (accessed 29 November 2005).

——(2004) 'Earth democracy', in R. Albritton, S. Bell, J. R. Bell and R. Westra (eds) *New Socialisms: futures beyond globalization*, London: Routledge.

——(2005) *India Divided: diversity and democracy under attack*, New York: Seven Stories Press.

Shiva, V., Bandyopadhyay, J., Pandurang, H., Krishnamurthy, B. V., Kurien, J., Narendranath, G., Ramprasad, V. and Reddy, S. T. S. (1991) *Ecology and the Politics of Survival: conflicts over natural resources in India*, New Delhi: United Nations University Press; New Delhi: Sage.

Short, J. (1984) 'The social fabric of risk: towards the social transformation of risk analysis', *American Sociological Review*, 49: 711–25.

Smith, C. (1998) *Creative Britain*, London: Faber & Faber.

Solow, R. (1970) *Growth Theory: an exposition*, Oxford: Clarendon Press.

Spicer, A. and Jones, C. (2004) 'Entrepreneurial excess', in J. Brewis, S. Linstead, D. Boje and A. O'Shea (eds) *Passion of Organizing*, Copenhagen: Copenhagen Business School Press. Online. Available: www.le.ac.uk/ulmc/doc/cjones_excess.pdf (accessed 7 September 2005).

Sprinker, M. (ed.) (1999) *Ghostly Demarcations: a symposium on Jacques Derrida's Specters of Marx*, London: Verso.

Stehr, N. (2001) 'Modern societies as knowledge societies', in G. Ritzer and B. Smart (eds) *Handbook of Social Theory*, London: Sage.

Stiglitz, J. E. (1999) 'Knowledge as a global public good', in I. Kaul, I. Grunberg and M. A. Stern (eds) *Global Public Goods: international cooperation in the 21st Century*, Oxford: Oxford University Press.

—— (2002) *Globalization and its Discontents*, London: Penguin.

Strathern, M. (ed.) (2000) *Audit Cultures: anthropological studies in accountability, ethics and the academy*, European Association of Social Anthropologists, London: Routledge.

Takagi, T. (1997) *Reading the Future: Japanese information services*, East Asian Library Resources Group of Australia Newsletter, No. 33. Online. Available: http://coombs.anu.edu.au/SpecialProj/NLA/EALRGA/newsletters97/970302.Takagi.html (accessed 5 September 2005).

Testart, A. (1998) 'Uncertainties of the "obligation to reciprocate": a critique of Mauss', in W. James and N. J. Allen (eds) *Marcel Mauss: a centenary tribute*, New York: Berghahn.

Third World Network (TWN) (2005) Website. Online. Available: www.twnside.org.sg/index.htm (accessed 29 November 2005).

Toffler, A. (1980) *The Third Wave: the classic study of tomorrow*, New York: Bantam Books.

Touraine, A. (1974) *The Post-industrial Society: tomorrow's social history: classes, conflicts and culture in programmed society*, New York: Wildwood House (French version 1971).

Trewin, D. (2002) *Measuring a Knowledge-based Economy and Society: an Australian framework*, Canberra: Australian Bureau of Statistics/Commonwealth of Australia.

Tsiolkas, C. (2005a) *Dead Europe*, Milsons Point, NSW: Vintage.

—— (2005b) Interview. Online. Available: www.paperbackbooks.com.au/christos.htm#interview (accessed 17 May 2006).

Tulloch, J. and Lupton, D. (2003) *Risk and Everyday Life*, London: Sage.

UNESCO (2003) *Knowledge Society vs. Knowledge Economy*. Online. Available: http://portal.unesco.org/education/ev.php-URL_ID=21012& URL_DO=DO_TOPIC&URL_SECTION=201 (accessed 17 January 2004).

Valaskakis, K. (1979) *The Information Society: the issues and the choices; integrating report for the information society project*, Ottawa: Department of Communications.

Velterop, J. M. (2005) *Open Access Publishing and Scholarly Societies: a guide*, New York: Open Society Institute.

Watkins, P. (1994) 'The Fordist/post-Fordist debate: the educational implications', in J. Kenway (ed.) *Economising Education: the post-Fordist directions*, Geelong, Australia: Deakin University.

Watson, D. (2003) *Death Sentence: the decay of public language*, Milsons Point, NSW: Random House Australia.
Webster, F. (1995) *Theories of the Information Society*, New York: Routledge.
Weiner, A. B. (1992) *Inalienable Possessions: the paradox of keeping-while-giving*, Berkeley, CA: University of California Press.
Wenzel, G. (1999) 'Traditional ecological knowledge and Inuit: reflections on TEK research and ethics', *Arctic*, 52(2): 113–24.
White, L. (1978) *Medieval Technology and Social Change*, Oxford: Oxford University Press.
Wikipedia (2005) 'Biopiracy'. Online. Available: http://en.wikipedia.org/wiki/Biopiracy (accessed 26 November 2005).
Williams, J. (1998) *Lyotard: towards a postmodern philosophy*, Cambridge: Polity.
——(2000) *Lyotard and the Political*, London: Routledge.
Wilson, S. (2002) *Information Arts: intersections of art, science and technology*, Cambridge, MA: MIT Press.
Winston, B. (1998) *Media Technology and Society. A history: from the telegraph to Internet*, London: Routledge.
World Bank (2005) *Knowledge for Development [K4D]*, Online. Available: http://web.worldbank.org/WBSITE/EXTERNAL/WBI/WBIPROGRAMS/KFDLP/0,contentMDK:20269026~menuPK:461205~pagePK:64156158~piPK:64152884~theSitePK;461198,00.html (accessed 1 September 2005).
Yan, Y. (2002) 'Unbalanced reciprocity: asymmetrical gift giving and social hierarchy in rural China', in M. Osteen (ed.) *The Question of the Gift: essays across disciplines*, London: Routledge.
Yūjirō, H. (1969) *Jōhōka Shakai: hado na shakai kara sofuto na shakai e (The Information Society)*, Tokyo: Kodansha.
Zicker, J. P. (1999) 'Survival economy and core-periphery dynamics in the Taimyr Autonomous Region, Russia', *Anthropology of East Europe Review*, 17(2). Online. Available: http://condor.depaul.edu/rorrotenbe/aeer/v17n2/Zicker.pdf (accessed 20 August 2004).
Zurr, I. and Catts, O. (2003) 'Are the semi-living semi-good or semi-evil?', *Technoetic Arts: An International Journal of Speculative Research*, 1. Online. Available: www.tca.uwa.edu.au/atGlance/pubMainFrames.html (accessed 4 November 2004).

Index